An Introduction to
Biblical Aramaic

An Introduction to
Biblical Aramaic

Andreas Schuele

WJK WESTMINSTER
JOHN KNOX PRESS
LOUISVILLE · KENTUCKY

© 2012 Andreas Schuele

First edition
Published by Westminster John Knox Press
Louisville, Kentucky

14 15 16 17 18 19 20 21—10 9 8 7 6 5 4 3 2

Book design by Sharon Adams
Cover design by Dilu Nicholas
Cover illustration: © Zadvinskiy and Jamie Farrant / istockphoto.com

Library of Congress Cataloging-in-Publication Data

Schuele, Andreas.
    An Introduction to Biblical Aramaic / Andreas Schuele.
        p.   cm.
    ISBN 978-0-664-23424-9 (alk. paper)
    1. Aramaic language—Grammar.   2. Aramaic language—Grammar—Examinations, questions, etc.   I. Title.
    PJ5213.S38   2012
    492'.29—dc23

                                                                    2012011410

♾ The paper used in this publication meets the minimum requirements of the American National Standard for Information Sciences—Permanence of Paper for Printed Library Materials, ANSI Z39.48-1992.

Most Westminster John Knox Press books are available at special quantity discounts when purchased in bulk by corporations, organizations, and special-interest groups. For more information, please e-mail SpecialSales@wjkbooks.com.

Contents

About This Book

Like most, if not all, Aramaic instructors, I have been deeply indebted to Franz Rosenthal's seminal *Grammar of Biblical Aramaic,* arguably the most comprehensive reference grammar available. At the same time, I found myself—again, probably like most of my colleagues—developing my own charts, summaries, and exercises in order to *introduce* students to Biblical Aramaic, rather than just to review the grammar for them. In accordance with the basic structure of a reference grammar, this book's purpose is to acquaint students with the writing system, phonology, morphology, and syntax of the pertinent texts in the books of Daniel and Ezra. It is a book primarily for the classroom and only secondarily for the specialists in Semitic linguistics. As such, it also seeks to account for the fact that most students who come to Biblical Aramaic have had prior exposure to Biblical Hebrew. While this introduction does not presuppose any particular level of expertise in Hebrew, it gives students the opportunity to relate what they know about Hebrew to their study of Aramaic. For this purpose, side glances at Biblical Aramaic's "big brother" complement the grammar discussion throughout the book.

Inasmuch as this introduction is a book *for* the classroom it is also a book *from* the classroom. The decisions about what to unfold in detail and what to mention in passing were profoundly influenced by what students found to be challenging aspects of the language. Apart from the particularities of Aramaic nouns and verbs, this led me to place special emphasis on syntactical issues. Biblical Aramaic is both a uniquely idiomatic and a highly formulaic language, which means that, even more than in Hebrew, the ability to parse forms is only the first step toward understanding the meaning of sentences and entire texts.

The reader should note that I refer throughout to the Masoretic versification, which, in the book of Daniel, differs from the English versions in the following places: Eng. 4:1–3 = MT 3:31–33; Eng. 4:4–37 = MT 4:1–34; Eng. 5:31 = MT 6:1; Eng. 6:2–28 = MT 6:2–29. Unless otherwise noted, the translations of all texts are my own.

Finally a word of thanks. I am grateful to Westminster John Knox Press for including a technical book like this in their program. My hope is that this will help to cultivate an awareness in the church that thorough linguistic training is not a luxury reserved for the academic guild but rather an indispensible part of the training of those who seek to become interpreters of Scripture.

Abbreviations

abs.	absolute (state)
adj.	adjective
BA	Biblical Aramaic
BH	Biblical Hebrew
c.	common
cent(s).	century(ies)
cf.	compare
const.	construct (state)
dem.	demonstrative
det.	determinate (state)
f.	feminine
ha.	Hapᶜel (conjugation)
hitpa.	Hitpaᶜᶜal (conjugation)
hitpe.	Hitpeᶜel (conjugation)
ho.	Hopᶜal (conjugation)
impf.	imperfect
impv.	imperative
inf.	infinitive
lit.	literal(ly)
m.	masculine
m.l.	mater lectionis
n.e.	*nun energicum* (energic *nun*)
neg.	negation/negative
NRSV	New Revised Standard Version
pa.	Paᶜᶜel (conjugation)
pe.	Peᶜal (conjugation)
pf.	perfect

pl.	plural
prep.	preposition
pron.	pronoun
ptc.	participle
reg.	regular
RSV	Revised Standard Version
sg.	singular
suf.	suffix

What Is "Biblical Aramaic"?

The term *Biblical Aramaic* points to the fact that, in addition to Biblical Hebrew, the Old Testament/Hebrew Bible hosts one other Semitic language. Parts of the books of Daniel (Dan 2:4–7:28) and Ezra (4:8–6:18; 7:12–26), as well as one verse from the book of Jeremiah (Jer 10:11) and two words in Genesis 31:47 were written in Aramaic. The pertinent passages in Daniel and Ezra seem to have been consciously inserted into literary contexts that otherwise used Hebrew (cf. Dan 2:4 and Ezra 4:7). The reason for the change of language is apparent in Ezra: these texts include correspondence between Jewish officials and the Persian court. Although exegetes dispute if or to what extent these are authentic documents, it is clear that at the time of the Persian Empire any correspondence between a province and the royal court, whether authentic or imaginary, had to be in Aramaic, the lingua franca. It is the literary genre itself that calls for Aramaic. However, in the book of Daniel, there is no obvious reason why the language changes from Hebrew to Aramaic and then returns to Hebrew in chapter 8. According to one hypothesis, the text of Daniel as we have it in the Hebrew Bible is an unfinished translation from Aramaic into Hebrew. This view is based on the assumption that, by the time the book was composed (in the first half of the 2nd cent. BCE), Hebrew had already been recognized as the language of the canonical traditions, whereas Aramaic had become the dominant spoken and written language. But such an explanation may not be required. Most likely, the Daniel tradition, which, as the Greek transmission shows, extended well beyond the biblical material, comprised texts in both Hebrew and Aramaic that were then included in the biblical book of Daniel.

On linguistic grounds, *Biblical Aramaic* is a bit of an awkward category. Although dating and locating the Ezra and Daniel texts is tricky, most exegetes agree that there may be more than two centuries between Ezra and most of Daniel, and that not only time but also space separates them. Ezra's frame of reference is the rebuilding of the temple in Jerusalem, while Daniel's world is that of the Babylonian Diaspora. Despite these striking differences in context, the language used in both traditions is relatively similar. Because of their genre as folktales, the Daniel narratives exhibit an Aramaic that is more idiomatic than Ezra's, but there are hardly any differences in morphology and syntax. This can be explained by the fact that the language of both Ezra and Daniel is part of what Semitists call *Imperial* (or *Official*) *Aramaic*. By the late Assyrian and Babylonian periods Aramaic, rather than cuneiform, was being used in the official communication between Mesopotamia and Syria-Palestine. In the Persian period, Aramaic finally advanced to the status of the lingua franca, the common language of the Achaemenid Empire. If it was ever true in early antiquity that the earth had the same language and the same words, as Genesis 11:1 depicts it, then this was Imperial Aramaic. This does not mean that there was only one spoken language at that time. People certainly continued to use their native languages and local dialects. However, the remarkable degree of coherence of the texts that have come to us from this period can be attributed to the use of Aramaic as the standard written language—not unlike medieval Latin or even today's common English. An introduction to Biblical Aramaic, therefore, provides access not only to the pertinent texts in Ezra and Daniel but also to the literary remnants of the Persian period[1] and beyond. Even the Aramaic texts from Qumran[2] (mostly from the 2nd and 1st cents. BCE), despite their particularities, are still indebted to Imperial Aramaic as their predecessor. It is only toward the end of the first millennium BCE and in the following centuries that two grammatically distinct types of Aramaic emerge: an Eastern type (in Mesopotamia) and a Western type (in Syria-Palestine).[3]

---

1. Cf. the vast amount of epigraphic material from Egypt, especially the documents from Elephantine (today's Aswan), where a Jewish military colony was stationed during the Achaeminid period. See B. Porten, ed., *Jews of Elephantine and Arameans of Syene: Fifty Aramaic Texts with Hebrew and English Translations* (Jerusalem: Hebrew University, 1976); B. Porten and A. Yardeni, *Textbook of Aramaic Documents from Ancient Egypt,* 4 vols. (Jerusalem: Hebrew University, 1986–1999). One document that needs to be mentioned in particular for its historical importance is the *Behistun* (or Bisitun) inscription of King Darius. It exists in three different versions: Old Persian, Akkadian, and Aramaic. See J. C. Greenfield and B. Porten, eds., *The Bisitun Inscription of Darius the Great: Aramaic Version,* Corpus Inscriptionum Iranicarum (London: Lund Humphries, 1982).

2. For editions cf. K. Beyer, *Die aramäischen Texte vom Toten Meer,* 2 vols. (Göttingen: Vandenhoeck & Ruprecht, 1984–2004); J. H. Charlesworth, ed., *The Dead Sea Scrolls: Hebrew, Aramaic, and Greek Texts with English Translations* (Louisville: Westminster John Knox, 1994–).

3. An overview of the history of Aramaic is provided by K. Beyer, *The Aramaic Language: Its Distribution and Subdivisions,* trans. J. F. Healey (Göttingen: Vandenhoeck & Ruprecht, 1986).

From the Phoenician to the Aramaic Writing System

CONSONANTS AND SYLLABLES

The inventors of the Northwest Semitic writing system were the Phoenicians, who had lived in the northern coastal area of Syria-Palestine long before Arameans and Canaanites (among them especially Moabites, Ammonites, Edomites, and eventually Israelites and Judeans) settled in the same area. Compared especially with the much more sophisticated cuneiform system of Mesopotamia, the Phoenician system presents a rather handy and easy-to-learn alphabet. It consists of twenty-two signs, the same as in the Hebrew alphabet (see comparison table on p. 4).

This writing system had its merits. It was easier to learn and to use than cuneiform, which required a much greater level of scribal sophistication and expertise. However, since it includes only consonants, the simplicity of the Phoenician script involved a significant level of ambiguity regarding the vocalization and meaning of words. A simple form like פעל can have a variety of grammatical functions and meanings: infinitive, all imperative forms (except f. pl.), 3rd masculine or feminine singular perfect, 3rd plural perfect, singular participle (all forms), plural participle (const.). Although these possibilities are never equally likely in a given literary context, the writing of consonants alone requires the reader to complete the phonemic structure of a word. This is certainly not a specific problem of Northwest Semitic languages, since no writing system (except perhaps the International Phonetic Alphabet) could ever represent the entire phonemic inventory of a given language. However, it seems that the lack of any vowel signs was perceived as a problem, at least by those who adopted the Phoenician writing system.

Original form	Square script
⋌	א
𝟡	ב
ר	ג
△	ד
⋑	ה
Y	ו
I	ז
Ħ	ח
⊕	ט
⇃	י
Ψ	כ / ך
⟨	ל
៣	מ / ם
⑂	נ / ן
∓	ס
O	ע
⌐	פ / ף
Ͱ	צ / ץ
Ϙ	ק
ⴌ	ר
W	ש
X	ת

The Phoenicians themselves never changed or developed their script. Significant changes occurred, however, when the Arameans took it over and adjusted it to the needs of their own language. The most significant novelty that the Arameans introduced was *vowel signs* (also called *matres lectionis*, "reading aids"); they used some of the signs (א, ה, י, and ו) to indicate vowels. This was probably not a deliberate invention but resulted from the coming together of the Phoenician script and Aramaic phonetics. For example, the Arameans pronounced פנמו (a Phoenician personal name) *Panamū*, whereas the Phoenicians themselves pronounced it *Panamuwa*. To the Arameans, the ו in פנמו was not a consonant but a symbol expressing the final *-ū*. So it was to a certain extent by coincidence that the Arameans introduced vowel signs to the Phoenician script.

Originally, these vowel signs were used only for long vowels at the ends of words. At a later stage, however, they were increasingly used in the cores of words and for short vowels, as the Qumran texts especially show (חוכמתא אוצרת, "The treasures of wisdom"; the ו in אוצרת indicates a long (and in this case contracted) vowel [ʾawṣār > ʾōṣār]; in חוכמתא, however, the vowel is short [ḥokmātāʾ] and would not have been written in Old/Ancient/Early Aramaic texts).

THE DEVELOPMENT OF SPECIFIC PHONEMES IN ARAMAIC AND HEBREW

Vowel signs are a genuine feature of the Aramaic script. They are familiar to students who know Hebrew before they come to Aramaic. Historically, however, it was the other way round: when the Palestinian tribes settled down, they took over the writing system from their immediate neighbors, the Arameans.

A problem for the Arameans was that the Phoenician alphabet did not match entirely the phonemic inventory of their language. In particular, the Arameans had more consonants than the Phoenicians, which meant that some signs had to be used for more than one consonantal value. The following chart indicates those cases where, for reasons to be explained below, a consonant expressed two or three different phonemes.[4]

---

4. One of the texts that provide insight into this stage of the development of Aramaic is the royal inscription of King Zakkur of Hamat, which dates from the 9th cent. BCE. A portion of this inscription is included in appendix 1 of this book.

Old Aramaic	
א	ʾ
ב	b
ג	g
ד	d
ה	h
ו	w
ז	z, ḏ
ח	ḥ, ḫ
ט	ṭ
י	y
כ	k
ל	l
מ	m
נ	n
ס	s
ע	ʿ, r[5]
פ	p
צ	ṣ, tˢ
ק	q, ḡ
ר	r
ש	š, ś, ṯ
ת	t

But how does one know about multiple consonantal values, if there is only one sign? This becomes clear if one compares Old Aramaic with another Semitic language, such as Biblical Hebrew. A few rules help us to understand why certain words are spelled differently in Hebrew than in Aramaic, although they are the same words.

ז

Besides the soft sibilant /z/, as in English "zoo," ז also represented the interdental /ḏ/, as the *th* in "those." It is called "interdental" because it has a

---

5. A deep laryngeal, rolled /r/.

sibilant (*s*-like) and a dental (*d/t*-like) component. For example, the masculine singular demonstrative pronoun "this (one)" was originally spelled זִי and pronounced /ḏī/. In later Aramaic (including BA), the same word was spelled differently, namely דִי. This suggests that the pronunciation had changed to /dī/. The *interdental* had become purely *dental*. Ancient Hebrew had the same interdental but here it turned into a *sibilant*; the word זה was still written with a ז but pronounced /zæ/.

The practical rule for students who are already familiar with Hebrew is that in some cases (where ancient Northwest Semitic had an interdental) BA shows a ד, while BH has a ז.

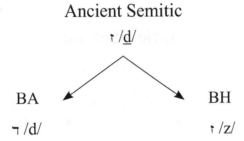

Ancient Semitic

ז /ḏ/

BA   BH

ד /d/   ז /z/

This includes the following words:

	BA	**BH**
"gold"	דְּהַב	זָהָב
"altar"	מַדְבַּח	מִזְבֵּחַ
"arm"	דְּרָע	זְרוֹעַ
"to sacrifice"	דְּבַח	זָבַח

צ

The same principle of interdentals splitting up into a dental component (Aramaic) and a sibilant component (Hebrew) applies to /t̠ˢ/, a consonant that has no equivalent in English (one would have to pronounce /ts/ and /th/ at the same time). In Aramaic this interdental eventually became an emphatic /ṭ/ (nonexistent in English), written ט; in Hebrew it became an emphatic /ṣ/ (as in "tsetse fly"), written צ.

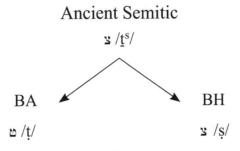

Ancient Semitic

צ /t̠ˢ/

BA   BH

ט /ṭ/   צ /ṣ/

Examples

	BA	**BH**
"mountain"	טוּר	צוּר
"summer"	קַיִט	קַיִץ

שׁ

A third case of interdentals becoming dentals and sibilants is /ṯ/, such as the *th* in "thing" or "therapy." In Aramaic this developed into a simple /t/, written ת, in Hebrew into a /š/, as in "ship," written שׁ.

Ancient Semitic

שׁ /ṯ/

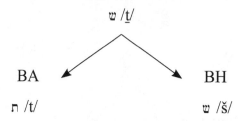

BA   BH

ת /t/   שׁ /š/

Examples

	BA	**BH**
"three"	תְּלָת	שָׁלֹשׁ
"to return"/"to do again"	תּוּב	שׁוּב
"to sit/settle down"	יְתַב	יָשַׁב

ק

A final case where Aramaic and Hebrew developed different consonantal values from the same ancient Northwest Semitic phoneme is an emphatic laryngeal whose original pronounciation, again, is uncertain. The most important word that includes this sound is "land," in Old Aramaic written ארק (as in Jer 10:11). Students of Hebrew know this word as ארץ (אֶרֶץ). The original sound seems to have had an emphatic sibilant component that in Hebrew merged with צ, whereas in later (Biblical) Aramaic it merged with ע and became ארע (אֲרַע).

Ancient Semitic

ק /ḡ/

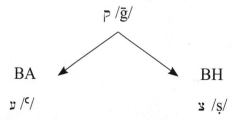

BA   BH

ע /ʿ/   צ /ṣ/

Examples

	BA	**BH**
"land"	אֲרַע	אֶרֶץ
"wool"	עֲמַר	צֶמֶר

Eventually, the alphabet of Imperial Aramaic comprised twenty-two signs that stood for twenty-three consonants (only שׁ still expressed two consonantal values: [š] and [ś]).

BA	
א	ꞌ
ב	b
ג	g
ד	d
ה	h
ו	w
ז	z
ח	ḥ
ט	ṭ
י	y
כ	k
ל	l
מ	m
נ	n
ס	s
ע	ꞥ
פ	p
צ	ṣ
ק	q
ר	r
שׁ	š, ś
ת	t

Masoretic Vowel Signs

Whereas BA texts represent the consonants of Imperial Aramaic, vowel signs were added to these texts at a much later stage by the Tiberian Masoretes (8th to 10th cents. CE). As with BH, more than a millennium lies between the consonants and the addition of vowel signs. The Masoretes applied a vocalizing system that, in their view, represented the Aramaic vowels of the ancient texts. However, since the Masoretes themselves spoke Aramaic, there is reason to assume that, to a large extent, the Masoretes' vocalization of BA reflects the Aramaic of their own time.

The Masoretes distinguished between *stops* and *spirants* for the following six consonants: ב, ג, ד, כ, פ, and ת (the so-called **begadkepat** consonants). The stop pronounciation (b, g, d, k, p, t) is indicated by a *dagesh lene* (בּ, גּ, דּ, כּ, פּ, תּ) and applies when no vowel precedes the consonant: בְּרִיךְ "blessed" (beginning of a word), מַלְכָּא "the king" (*mal-kāʾ*, no vowel before כ). If a vowel stands before one of these consonants, they are spirantized and written without a *dagesh*: אַב "father," עָבֵד "making" (vowels precede both the ב and the ד). For the purpose of reading it is not crucial to distinguish between stop and spirant. One can pronounce these consonants either as stops, regardless of whether they carry a *dagesh*, or use the Modern Hebrew pronounciation that distinguishes between stop and spirant only in the cases of ב (/b/ or /v/), כ (/k/ or /k̲/), and פ (/p/ or /f/).[6]

The *dagesh* sign can also indicate the *doubling* of a consonant (מִלָּה "word," הִמּוֹ "they"); in these cases, it is called a *dagesh forte*. All consonants can be doubled except the laryngeals (or gutturals): א, ה, ח, ע, and ר. Note that for the **begadkepat** this means that a *dagesh* can be either a *dagesh forte* (קַדִּישׁ *qaddîš*

---

6. For the remaining three consonants the spirant pronounciations are /θ/ (ת) as in "thick," /th/ (ד) as in "those," and /ġ/ (ג), a laryngeal *r*-like sound.

10

"holy," חֲנֻכָּה *ḥănūkkâ* "consecration") or a *dagesh lene*; in נַּפַּיִן *gappîn* "wings," the *dagesh* in נ is a *dagesh lene*, whereas in פ it is a *dagesh forte*.

VOWELS AND VOWEL SIGNS

The three basic vowels in most of the ancient Semitic languages are *a*, *i*, and *u*. They are either long or short. Other vowels can be seen as filling the phonic spectrum between *a*/*i* and *a*/*u*.

Long vowels

$$\bar{a}$$

$$\bar{e} \qquad \bar{o}$$

$$\bar{\imath} \qquad \qquad \bar{u}$$

The Masoretic names of these vowels are:

$\bar{a}$ *qāmeṣ*, $\bar{e}$ *ṣērê*, $\bar{\imath}$ (long) *ḥīreq*, $\bar{o}$ *ḥōlem*, $\bar{u}$ (long) *qibbûṣ*

Short vowels

$$a$$

$$e \ (\text{æ}) \qquad o \ (\text{ŏ})$$

$$i \qquad \qquad u$$

a *pataḥ*, e (æ) *sĕgōl*, i (short) *ḥīreq*, o (ŏ) *qāmeṣ ḥāṭûp*, u (short) *qibbûṣ*

The vowel signs are identical with those of BH:

qāmeṣ	$\bar{a}$	בָ
qāmeṣ ḥaṭûp[7]	o	בָ
pataḥ	a	בַ
sĕgōl	e	בֶ
ṣērê	$\bar{e}$	בֵ
ḥīreq	i/$\bar{\imath}$	בִ
qibbûṣ	u/$\bar{u}$	בֻ
ḥōlem	$\bar{o}$	בֹ

7. As in BH, the *qāmeṣ* sign can also stand for the *qāmeṣ ḥāṭûp* (short open *o* as in "obstacle") in closed syllables that do not carry the main emphasis of the word. For example, in חָכְמָה (*ḥokmâ*) "wisdom" the emphasis is on the last syllable. The first *qāmeṣ* does not have an emphasis and occurs in a closed syllable; thus it is a *qāmeṣ ḥāṭûp*.

According to the Masoretic system, there are "long" and "over-long" (or "ultra-long") syllables. A long syllable can be an open syllable, consisting of a *consonant + long vowel* (*bā, mī, kū*), or a closed syllable, consisting of a *consonant + short vowel + closing consonant* (*bab, min, kul*). A syllable is over-long if it is closed and has a long vowel (*bāb, mīn, kūl*).

However, there are also examples of open syllables with short vowels (*ba, mi, ku*), for example, אֲבִי (two syllables: אֲ-בִי, *ʾa-bî* "my father"), in which case the Masoretes usually add an accent (*metheg*) to the short syllable in order to lengthen it.

The Masoretes also created a set of signs to indicate where there was no full vowel or no vowel at all. Except for the laryngeals א, ה, ח, and ע, the sign for a "semi-vowel" or "half-vowel" is the *vocal shewa*[8] (or, using Latin, *shewa mobile*) (e.g., בְּ, transliterated *bĕ-*).[9] Since the *vocal shewa* is not a full vowel, it cannot stand in an open syllable on its own. Thus the consonant carrying the *shewa* is an upbeat or reduced syllable to the following full syllable: שְׁלָם *šĕlām* or *šĕ-lām* "wellbeing."

However, the Masoretes also used the *shewa* sign to indicate the *end* of a closed syllable: קִרְיָא (קִרְ-יָא) *qir-yāʾ* "city," חָכְמָה (חָכְ-מָה) *ḥok-mâ* "wisdom." In these cases, the *shewa* is silent and thus called *silent shewa* or *shewa quiescens*.

These rules are roughly the same in BA and BH. The following list includes Aramaic words analyzed according to their syllabic structure:

דִּין	"judgment"	דִּין (one closed syllable)
שִׁמְעֵת	"I have heard"	שִׁמְ - עֵת (two closed syllables, first one with *silent shewa*)
בְּמַלְכוּתָךְ	"in your kingdom"	בְּמַלְ - כוּ - תָךְ (1. closed syllable, ending with *silent*[10] *shewa*; 2. open syllable; 3. closed syllable)
חַרְטֻמִּין	"magicians"	חַרְ - טֻמּ - מִין (1. closed syllable, ending with *silent shewa*; 2. closed syllable;[11] 3. closed syllable)

8. We will be using the transliteration *shewa*, which most textbooks prefer, instead of *šᵉwā* or *schwa*.

9. Sometimes also transliterated as *ə* or ᵉ.

10. Notice that even though the *shewa* is silent, the following *kaph* has no *dagesh*. This anomaly has been noted by scholars, but there is no good explanation. On occasion, the Masoretes apparently did not follow their own rules.

11. Note that the doubled מ counts as two consonants for the syllabic structure of the word.

גָלוּתָא	"the exile"	גָּ - לוּ - תָא (three open[12] syllables)
הֻעַלּוּ	"they were brought"	הֻ - עַל - לוּ (1. open syllable; 2. closed syllable; 3. open syllable[13])
הִשְׁתְּכַחַת	"it was found"	הִשׁ - תְּכַ - חַת (1. closed syllable with *silent shewa*; 2. open syllable, with *vocal shewa*; 3. closed syllable)
קִרְיְתָא	"the city"	קִר - יְתָא (1. closed syllable with *silent shewa*; 2. open syllable, with *vocal shewa*)
יִשְׁלַח	"he will send"	יִשׁ - לַח (1. closed syllable with *silent shewa*; 2. closed syllable)

In the case of the laryngeals (א, ה, ח, and ע) the Masoretes decided that the vocal *shewa* should have an *a*-like sound and thus put a *pataḥ*, *qāmeṣ*, or *sĕgōl* next to the *shewa* (בֲ / בֳ / בֱ). These are called *ḥāṭēp pataḥ*, *ḥāṭēp qāmeṣ*,[14] and *ḥāṭēp sĕgōl*.

אֱלָהָא	"God"	אֱלָ - הָא (1. open syllable, with *ḥāṭēp sĕgōl*; 2. open syllable
אֲמַרְנָא	"we said"	אֲמַר - נָא (1. closed syllable, with *ḥāṭēp pataḥ*, ending with *silent shewa*; 2. open syllable)
וּפַחֲוָתָא	"and the governors"	וּפַ - חֲוָ - תָא (1. open syllable, beginning with וּ;[15] 2. open syllable, with *ḥāṭēp pataḥ*; 3. open syllable)
קֳדָם	"before"	קֳדָם (1. closed syllable, with *ḥāṭēp qāmeṣ*)

12. Note that the aleph does not close the syllable, even though it is a consonant (here and in several examples to follow). In all these cases, aleph is m. l. for a long vowel at the end of a word (either feminine ending or article).

13. The doubled ל counts as two consonants.

14. The *ḥāṭēp qāmeṣ* has roughly the same pronounciation as the *qāmeṣ ḥāṭûp* (*o*). Note, however, that the *ḥāṭēp qāmeṣ* occurs only in open syllables, the *qāmeṣ ḥāṭûp* only in closed syllables.

15. Note that the conjunction וְ or וּ "and" is considered part of the word (noun or verb) to which it is attached and as such "lengthens" the opening syllable.

Exercise 1: Syllabic Structure of BA Words

Analyze the syllabic structure of the following words.

מַלְכִין	"kings"	
כָּהֲנָא	"priest"	
שְׁמַיָּא	"heaven"	
אַרְבְּעָה	"four"	
גַּלְגִּלּוֹהִי	"its wheels"	
הִתְנַבִּי	"he prophesied"	
יִתְרְמֵא	"he shall be cast"	

אַרְגְּוָנָא	"purple"	
לְהַשְׁכָּחָה	"in order to find"	

It is important to realize that the rules for pointing words in BA are even less systematic than in BH. As with all the ancient Semitic languages written in the Phoenician alphabet, it is helpful to first develop a sense of the consonantal patterns, since the Masoretic vowel signs are a later addition to, but not a part of, the original text.

DIFFERENCES BETWEEN ARAMAIC AND HEBREW VOWELS

For students who come to BA from BH, a few observations help us understand the differences between the systems of vowels in both languages.

Observation 1

Sometimes BH has a *ḥōlem* where BA has a *qāmeṣ*. In these cases, BA is closer to the original Northwest Semitic vowel pattern than BH, which shifted *ā* to *ō/ô*.

	BA	BH
"human/humankind"	אֱנָשׁ	אֱנוֹשׁ
"generation"	דָּר	דֹּר, דּוֹר
"sound, voice"	קָל	קוֹל
"killing" (ptc.)	קָטֵל	קוֹטֵל

Observation 2

Unlike BH, BA has very few *segolate* nouns[16] (e.g., BH כֶּסֶף "silver, money"). The singular absolute forms of this group of nouns in BA have a vowel pattern *ĕ–a* (*shewa–patah*): כְּסַף "silver, money." There are a few exceptions to this rule, where the Hebrew and the Aramaic forms are identical: מֶלֶךְ "king," קֶרֶן "horn," and דְּתֵא "grass" (BH דֶּשֶׁא). It remains unclear whether these exceptions were made on purpose or if the Masoretes more or less unconsciously used the Hebrew patterns for the Aramaic as well.

Other examples include:

	BA	**BH**
"man," "a certain one"	גְּבַר	גֶּבֶר
"salt"	מְלַח	מֶלַח
"interpretation"	פְּשַׁר	פֵּשֶׁר
"meal," "feast"	לְחֵם	לֶחֶם
"servant"	עֲבַד	עֶבֶד
"wrath"	קְצַף	קֶצֶף

Observation 3

Unlike their vocalization of Hebrew words, the Masoretes did not lengthen vowels in pretonic syllables (syllables preceding the main emphasis of a word) in Aramaic. According to Masoretic rules, there should be no *open syllables* with a short vowel (e.g., *ba, mu, ki*). As a consequence, they had to either lengthen the vowel (consonant plus long vowel: *bā, mū, kī*) or they had to reduce it to a half-vowel (*shewa* or *ḥāṭēp* vowel: *bě, bǎ*). In pretonic syllables, the Masoretes chose *long vowels in Hebrew* and *half-vowels in Aramaic*:

1. Perfect 3 m. sg.: The original Northwest Semitic form was *qatál*. For the Hebrew, the Masoretes decided that the first (pretonic) sylla-ble should have a long vowel, קָטַל, whereas in Aramaic they reduced the vowel to *shewa*: קְטַל.
2. Nouns in the singular absolute state. Because there is no lengthening of originally short vowels in pretonic syllables, a large number of Aramaic nouns begin with *shewa* or *ḥāṭēp* vowels.

16. Originally, these were nouns with double consonance at the end (/*kasp*/ "money"). The Masoretes, however, decided to break up the double consonance by inserting a short vowel between the second and third consonants. Since this short vowal is typically a *segol* (or, with laryngeals, *ḥāṭēp patah*), this group of nouns is referred to as *segolate* nouns.

אֱלָהּ	"God"
שְׁמַיִן	"heaven"
חֱמָא	"anger, "rage"
קְצָת	"end," "part (of)"

Exercise 2: Aramaic and Hebrew Word Comparisons

Based on the Aramaic phonetic system as well as on the Masoretic vocalization rules outlined above, try to construct the Hebrew forms of the following BA words. Where there are no vowels, identify the three root consonants in Hebrew.

שְׁלָם		שֶׁמֶשׁ	
זְרַע		תבר	
חֲדַת		תּוֹר	
יעט		תְּלַג	
צְלֵם		כדב	

KETIB AND QERE

As in BH, the Masoretes decided to vocalize certain Aramaic words against the vocalization that the consonantal text itself suggests. It is not clear whether they wished to "correct" the written text (they obviously did not feel at liberty to change the sacred consonantal text itself) or if they intuitively used the vocalization (*qĕrê* "what is read") to which they were accustomed, although it did not always match the consonants that were written (*kĕtîb* "what is written"). For example, the consonants for "zither" are קיתרוס, which suggests that one should read קִיתָרוֹס (*qîtārôs* "guitar"). However, the Masoretes vocalize it קַיתְרוֹס (*qatrôs*), as if the י was not there.[17] In a number of Bible editions both the Qere and the Ketib are printed next to each other. Other editions, like the *Biblia Hebraica Stuttgartensia,* keep the original consonantal text together with the masoretic vowels. Other examples:

17. The most famous example of a Qere is the Tetragrammaton. יהוה follows the pattern of an imperfect form: *Yahweh.* The Masoretes, however, avoided pronouncing the divine name and used the vowels of the word אֲדֹנָי (*ʾădōnāy*) "Lord" instead. Note, however, that, while the Tetragrammaton occurs in the Hebrew sections of Daniel and Ezra, it is never used in the Aramaic passages of these books.

אַנְתָּה (BA 2 m. sg. pron.) "you." The Ketib אנתה suggests that one should read אַנְתָּה; the Masoretes vocalize it אַנְתְּ.

אֱנוֹשָׁא (BA m. sg. noun) "human being": Ketib אנושא (→אֱנוֹשָׁא); Qere אֲנָשָׁא.

The Noun

GENDER

Biblical Aramaic distinguishes between masculine and feminine forms; there is no third—neutral—gender. Where gender is grammatically expressed, the feminine singular ending, as in BH, is -*ā*. This can be indicated through ה- or less commonly (and unlike BH) א-.[18]

מֶלֶךְ	"king"
מַלְכָּה	"queen"
דִּין	"judgment" (m.)
מְדִינָה	"(judicial district =) province" (f.)
נְבִיא	"prophet" (m.)
נְבוּאָה	"prophecy" (f.)
חֵיוָא or חֵיוָה	"animal" (f.)

18. Note that in those cases where א- represents the feminine ending, it could mistakenly be interpreted as the Aramaic definite article (see below).

ABSOLUTE AND CONSTRUCT STATES

As in most Semitic languages, Aramaic has an *absolute* and a *construct* state. The absolute state indicates that a noun is not determined by any other noun, whereas in the construct state it is followed by one or several other nouns (genitive, or construct chain). For example, in the phrase "the house of David," "house" is the construct noun because it is determined in this case by a proper noun that explains whose house it is.

Whereas the masculine singular forms show no difference in the absolute and construct states, there are specific endings for the absolute and construct in the feminine singular and all of the plural forms.

Endings

	absolute	construct
m. sg.		
f. sg.	הָ ָ-/ אָ ָ-	ת ַ-
m. pl.	ין ִ-[19]	י ֵ-
f. pl.	ן ָ-	ת ָ-[20]

Paradigm

	absolute	construct
m. sg.	מֶלֶךְ	מֶלֶךְ
f. sg.[21]	מַלְכָּה	מַלְכַּת
m. pl.	מַלְכִין	מַלְכֵי-
f. pl.	מַלְכָן	מַלְכָת[22]

Examples

מַתְּנָן	"gifts" (sg. מַתְּנָה)
מָרֵא מַלְכִין	"the lord of kings"
מְדִינַת בָּבֶל	"the province of Babylon"
נְבוּאַת חַגַּי	"the prophecy of Haggai" (abs. נְבוּאָה "prophecy")

---

19. Cf. the Hebrew pl. ending ים- (-*îm*).

20. Cf. the Hebrew pl. ending וֹת- (-*ôt*) where the Aramaic form has אָ- (-*ʾā*).

21. There are, however, fem. nouns that do not have the fem. endings in the sg.; for example, רוּחַ "spirit," קֶרֶן "horn," אֶבֶן "stone."

22. Note that the only difference between the fem. sg. and pl. const. forms is the *pataḥ* in the sg. and the *qāmeṣ* in the pl.

חַכִּימִין	"wise men"
חַכִּימֵי בָבֶל	"the wise men of Babylon"
זְמָן	"(appointed) time" (sg.!; נ is part of the root)

The Determinate (Emphatic) State

The determinate (or emphatic) state denotes a noun *plus* the *definite article*. The form of the article in BA is unique. Whereas in Hebrew (and Arabic) the article precedes the word with which it is connected, it follows it in Aramaic as א ָ - (pronounced *ā*).

מַלְכָּא	"the king" (BH הַמֶּלֶךְ)
צְלֵם	"*a* statue/image"
צַלְמָא	"*the* statue/image"
בְּשַׂר	"flesh"
בִּשְׂרָא	"*the* flesh" (in Dan 2:11 meaning "humankind")
בֵּית־אֱלָהָא	"the house of God/the temple" (cf. BH בֵּית־הָאֱלֹהִים)

One possible explanation for the difference in the article is that in both Hebrew and Aramaic it was originally a deictic element הָא (*hāʾ*) "see (this)." In Hebrew it was placed before the word to which it referred. This eventually led to the assimilation of א to the first consonant of the following noun. This could be the reason why the article requires a doubling at the beginning of a word (*haʾ melek > hammelek*). In Aramaic the same deictic element was placed after the word, and the ה eventually disappeared so that only the א remained (*malk-hāʾ > malkāʾ*).

Unlike BH, the construct (not the absolute) forms provide the basis of the emphatic state.

Paradigm

m. sg.	מַלְכָּא	מלכ + א ָ
f. sg.	מַלְכְּתָא	מלכַת + א ָ
m. pl.	מַלְכַיָּא	מלכי + א ָ
f. pl.	מַלְכָתָא	מלכָת + א ָ[23]

23. Note that the only difference between the f. sg. and f. pl. are the vowels before the ending תא-.

It is important to be aware that the determinate state in BA is very common and can sometimes replace the absolute state without any change in meaning. Moreover, in many cases in BA one can only guess what the absolute form of a noun is because only the determinate form is attested. Also, sometimes the article can be written ה- instead of א-; this can be confusing, since, in these cases, a word looks like a feminine form: כְּתָבָא "the writing" is a determinate masculine form (abs. כְּתָב), but it can also be written כְּתָבָה.[24]

Exercise 3: Basic Noun Parsings

Parse and translate the following forms with the help of a dictionary.

שִׁמְשָׁא	יוֹמַיָּא
מְדִינְתָּא	חָכְמְתָא וּגְבוּרְתָא
נְבִזְבָּה	חֵיוָה
כָּהֲנַיָּא	שְׁאֵלְתָּא
שָׁלְטָנָא	פַּחֲוָתָא
תָּרְעַיָּא	שָׁעֲתָה
לִשָּׁנַיָּא	חֵיל שְׁמַיָּא
עֲרָוַת מַלְכָּא	שִׁלְטֹנֵי מְדִינָתָא

Particular Groups of Nouns

Nouns Ending in וּ- (-û) and יִ- (-î)

Absolute Singular

וּ- (-û) and, to a lesser extent, יִ - (-î), are common endings of *feminine* nouns. In many cases, these nouns are derived from roots ending in ה-.[25]

---

24. In Dan 5:7 and 15 both forms occur in each verse. Other words that have the article written as ה- sometimes as well as א- are מַלְכָּה "the king," and רָזָה "the mystery/riddle."

25. חֱזוּ "vision, appearance" (from חזה "to see") is another important noun ending in וּ-; in the plural, however, it has masculine forms: חֶזְוֵי רֵאשֵׁהּ "the visions of his head."

בָּעוּ	"prayer, request" (בעה "ask for, request")
רְבוּ	"greatness" (רבה "be/become great")
גָּלוּ	"exile" (גלה "uncover, reveal")
שָׁלוּ	"neglect" (שלה "be at ease, rest")
זָכוּ	"purity, innocence" (זכה "be pure, blameless")
רְעוּ	"pleasure, will" (רעה "to shepherd")
צְבוּ	"thing, matter"
נְוָלִי / נְוָלוּ	"dunghill, refuse heap"
אָחֳרִי	"another" (f.), probably derived from the m. form אָחֳרָן

Construct Singular

In the singular, the construct and determinate endings are simply added to the absolute ending וּ- (-û). In the construct forms, this is the standard feminine ending ת-, which leads to וּת- (e.g., בָּעוּת). As with other nouns, the construct form also provides the basis for the determinate state (e.g., גָּלוּתָא)[26] and pronominal suffixes (e.g., בָּעוּתֵהּ "his petition"; see below).

Determinate Singular

בְּנֵי־גָלוּתָא   "deportees" (lit. "the sons of the exile")

No absolute forms are attested in the plural.

Construct Plural

The וּ- turns into a full consonant, to which the feminine ending ת ָ- (-āt) is added.

מַלְכְוָת   "kingdoms of . . ."

Determinate Plural (const. form plus article)

כָּל־מַלְכְוָתָא   "all [other] kingdoms"

---

26. There are, however, exceptions. Sometimes the article can be attached to the absolute form, as in חֶזְוָא "the vision."

Nouns Ending in ה-

Another group of nouns that change their form in different states are those ending in ה-. As in most Semitic languages, a final ה is unstable and turns either into ו or י when followed by another consonant.

אַרְיֵה   "lion" (abs. sg.)

but

אַרְיָוָתָא   "the lions" (det. pl.)

מְעֵה (מְעָא)   "abdomen"

but

מְעַיִן   "entrails"

Important Individual Nouns

אַב "father"

The same ה- expansion of the word stem that one finds in שֵׁם/שְׁמָהָת also occurs in the plural (const.) of אַב: אֲבָהָת.[27]

בַּר "son"

בַּר has a different second consonant from the corresponding BH term בֵּן (*n* and *r*, however, belong to the same group of the so-called *liquid* consonants). In the plural forms, however, BA too has a *n*: בְּנִין (abs.), בְּנֵי-אֲנָשָׁא "humans."

כְּנָת "associate, partner"

A common Aramaic noun. In BA it occurs only in its plural construct form: כְּנָוָת.[28]

מִלָּה "word, matter"

מִלָּה covers about the same semantic field as BH דָּבָר. It has regular forms in the singular construct and determinate states (const. מִלַּת מַלְכָּא "the word of the king"; det. מִלְּתָא as in פְּשַׁר-מִלְּתָא "the interpretation of the matter"). Although it is a feminine noun, the plural endings are masculine: מִלִּין (abs.), מִלֵּי מַלְכָּא (const.), מִלַּיָּא (det.).

---

27. Attested are two suffixed forms: אֲבָהָתִי ("my ancestors") and אֲבָהָתַנָא ("our ancestors"). For nouns with suffixes see the next paragraph.

28. Attested is the suffixed form כְּנָוָתְהוֹן ("their associates").

שֵׁם "name"

Note the Aramaic vocalization שְׁם as opposed to BH שֵׁם. Although this is a masculine noun, the plural forms are gramatically feminine. Also, in the plural construct, the word stem has an additional ה: שְׁמָהָת (no other plural forms are attested).

Nouns with Suffixes

To express a possessional relationship (*your* mother, *my* nerves, etc.) BA uses pronominal suffixes, most of which are similar to those in BH. However, the suffixes of the third masculine singular (by far the most frequent of all pronominal suffixes in BA) show especially distinct forms.

	sg. noun + 3 m. sg. suf.	pl. noun + 3 m. sg. suf.
BH	בֵּיתוֹ	בָּנָיו
	"his house"	"his sons"
BA	בַּיְתֵהּ	בְּנוֹהִי

The pronominal suffixes of BA are the following:

	sg. noun	pl. noun
1 c. sg.	ִי	ַי
2 m. sg.	ָךְ	ָיךְ
3 m. sg.	ֵהּ	וֹהִי
3 f. sg.	ַהּ	ַיהּ
1 c. pl.	ַנָא	ַינָא
2 m. pl.	ְכֶן / ְכֹם	ֵיכֶן / ֵיכֹם
3 m. pl.	ְהֶן / ְהֹם	ֵיהֶן / ֵיהֹם
3 f. pl.	ְהֵן / ְהֵן[29]	ֵיהֵן / ֵיהֹם

---

29. The Ketiv indicates that the ending should be read ־הוֹן. The masoretic Qere, however, suggests a reading ־הֵן.

Suffixes attached to masculine nouns:

	sg. noun	pl. noun
1 c. sg.	אֱלָהִי "my god"	אֱלָהַי "my gods"
2 m. sg.	אֱלָהָךְ "your god"	אֱלָהָיִךְ "your gods"
3 m. sg.	אֱלָהֵהּ "his god"	אֱלָהוֹהִי "his gods"
3 f. sg.	אֱלָהַהּ "her god"	אֱלָהַיהַ "her gods"
1 c. pl.	אֱלָהַנָא "our god"	אֱלָהַינָא "our gods"
2 m. pl.	אֱלָהֲכֶם / אֱלָהֲכֶן "your god"	אֱלָהֵיכֶם / אֱלָהֵיכֶן "your gods"
3 m. pl.	אֱלָהֲהֶם / אֱלָהֲהֶן "their god"	אֱלָהֵיהֶם / אֱלָהֵיהֶן "their gods"
3 f. pl.	אֱלָהֲהֶן / אֱלָהֲהֶין "their god"	אֱלָהֵיהֶן / אֱלָהֵיהוּם "their gods"

In the case of feminine nouns, both singular and plural, the suffix is always attached to the ת- ending of the construct forms. This means that the suffixes added to the singular forms and those added to the plural forms do not differ.

Suffixes added to feminine nouns (note that, due to the small number of suffixed f. nouns, not all paradigmatic forms are attested):

	sg. noun	pl. noun
1 c. sg.	מַלְכַּתִי "my queen"	מַלְכָּתִי "my queens"
2 m. sg.	מַלְכַּתָךְ "your queen"	מַלְכָּתָךְ "your queens"
3 m. sg.	מַלְכַּתֵהּ "his queen"	מַלְכָּתֵהּ "his queens"
3 f. sg.	מַלְכַּתַהּ "her queen"	מַלְכָּתַהּ "her queens"
1 c. pl.	מַלְכַּתַנָא "our queen"	מַלְכָּתַנָא "our queens"
2 m. pl.	מַלְכַּתְכֶן / מַלְכַּתְכֶם "your queen"	מַלְכָּתְכֶן / מַלְכָּתְכֶם "your queens"
3 m. pl.	מַלְכַּתְהֶן / מַלְכַּתְהֶם "their queen"	מַלְכָּתְהֶן / מַלְכָּתְהֶם "their queens"
3 f. pl.	מַלְכַּתְהֶן / מַלְכַּתְהוּן "their queen"	מַלְכָּתְהֶן / מַלְכָּתְהוּן "their queens"

Examples

מַלְכוּתִי "my kingdom," רַעְיוֹנַי "my thoughts," כְּנָוָתְהוֹן "their associates," אֲבָהָתַנָא "our fathers," מִלְחַנָא "our salt," גַּוַּהּ "her midst," פֻּמַּהּ "its mouth," גַּלְגִּלּוֹהִי "its wheels," חֶלְמָךְ "your dream."

Exercise 4: Nouns with Suffixes

Identify the suffixes and translate the following words with the help of a dictionary.

אֲבָהָתִי	בְּרַהּ
קַרְצֵיהוֹן	רָאשֵׁיהֶם
נִשְׁמַהּ	שְׁגָלָתֵהּ
בָּתֵּיכוֹן	לִבְבָךְ
יְדָךְ	מַעְבָּדוֹהִי
אַתְרֵהּ	עֵינַי
שְׁמָהָתְהֹם	נִבְזְבְּיָתָךְ
עֲלִיתֵהּ	מַלְכוּתֵהּ

ADJECTIVES

Adjectives typically follow the noun to which they refer and match it in number and generally also in nominal state (absolute or determinate):

רוּחַ יַתִּירָה	"an excellent spirit" (f.)
יַמָּא רַבָּא	"the great sea"
אֱלָהִין קַדִּישִׁין	"holy gods"
אֱלָהָא עִלָּיָא	"the Most High God"
מַתְּנָן רַבְרְבָן שַׂגִּיאָן	"many great gifts"
חֵיוָה אָחֳרִי	"another beast"

In some cases (especially in metaphorical/descriptive language), the noun and its corresponding adjective are the subject and predicate of a nominal sentence:

אִילָן בְּגוֹא אַרְעָא וְרוּמֵהּ שַׂגִּיא

"(There was) a tree in the middle of the earth, and its height (was) *great*" (Dan 4:7)

עָפְיֵהּ שַׁפִּיר

"Its foliage (was) *beautiful*" (Dan 4:9)[30]

אָתוֹהִי כְּמָה רַבְרְבִין וְתִמְהוֹהִי כְּמָה תַּקִּיפִין

"How *great* (are) his signs, how *powerful* his wonders!"(lit. "His signs, how great, and his wonders, how powerful!"; Dan 3:33)

Especially in direct speech, adjectives can also serve as the predicate of a sentence where a noun is implied:

וְאָמְרִין לְמַלְכָּא יַצִּיבָא מַלְכָּא

"And they said to the king: 'Certainly [or: (this is) certainly so], O king!'" (Dan 3:24)

NUMERALS

Ordinal Numbers

Ordinal numbers typically have the ending יִ- (-āy): קַדְמָי "first, former" (m.), רְבִיעָיָה "fourth" (f.), and they are used in the same way as adjectives (usually following the noun and congruent in gender/number):

קַרְנַיָּא קַדְמָיָתָא	"the first horns"
קַדְמָיְתָא כְּאַרְיֵה	"the first (beast) was like a lion"
קַדְמָיֵא	"the former (ones)"
חֵיוָה תִנְיָנָה	"a second beast"
מַלְכוּ תְּלִיתָיָא	"a third kingdom"
חֵיוָה רְבִיעָיָה	"a fourth beast"

---

30. Given the relative scarcity of adjectives in BA, in some cases nouns function as adjectives, especially in nominal clauses: כָּל־מַעֲבָדוֹהִי קְשֹׁט וְאֹרְחָתֵהּ דִּין "All his deeds are true" (lit. "truth") and all his ways are just" (lit. "judgment"; Dan 4:34).

Cardinal Numbers

The following are attested in BA:

	m. abs.	m. const.	f. abs.	f. const.
1	חַד		חֲדָה	
2		תְּרֵי	תַּרְתֵּין	
	Note that for 3 to 10 the masculine cardinal numbers are connected with *feminine* nouns[31] and feminine numbers with *masculine* nouns.[32]			
3	תְּלָת		תְּלָתָה	
4	אַרְבַּע		אַרְבְּעָה	
5				
6	שֵׁת			
7			שִׁבְעָה	שִׁבְעַת
8				
9				
10	עֲשַׂר		עֲשְׂרָה	

31. קַרְנַיִן עֲשַׂר "ten horns" (קֶרֶן is f.!).
32. אַרְבְּעָה רֵאשִׁין "four heads."

For numbers above 10 the following are attested:

12	תְּרֵי עֲשַׂר
20	עֶשְׂרִין
30	תְּלָתִין
60	שִׁתִּין
100	מְאָה
200	מָאתַיִן (dual of 100)
400	אַרְבַּע מְאָה
1,000	אֲלַף (sg. abs.), אֶלֶף (sg. const.), אַלְפָּא (sg. det.)
thousands	אַלְפִּין (pl. of 1,000)
10,000	רִבּוֹ

GENTILICS

Like ordinal numbers, gentilics[33] have the ending יִ -ָ : פָּרְסָי "the Persian"; in the determinate state, the article is added to יָ -ָ > אָיָ -ָ. This suggests the pronunciation פַּרְסָיָא *parsāyā*. Note, however, that in a number of instances the Masoretes vocalize differently: פַּרְסָיָא *parsāʾā*. In this case, the Ketib (what is written) differs from the Qere (what is read).

The plural ending (abs.) is written ־אִין, which is usually pointed ־אִין ָ, as in כַּשְׂדָּאִין *kaśdāʾîn*; however, for the term "Judahites," the Masoretes also suggest the reading יְהוּדָאִין *yĕhûdāʾyîn*. A difference between the written text and the Masoretic vocalization also occurs in the plural determinate: the ending is ־אַיָ, which suggests the reading כַּשְׂדָּיֵא *kaśdāyēʾ*; the Masoretes, however, vocalize כַּשְׂדָּיֵא *kaśdāʾē*.

PREPOSITIONS

The BA prepositions and their meaning are mostly identical with those in BH. One-consonantal prepositions are attached to the referring noun; longer prepositions stand as separate words before the noun.

בְּ-

Spatial ("in," "at"): בְּבִקְעַת דּוּרָא בִּמְדִינַת בָּבֶל "in the plain of Dura, in the province of Babylon" (Dan 3:1)

---

33. Nouns that express national, ethnic, or religious affiliation.

Temporal ("in," "at"): בִּשְׁנַת חֲדָה "in the first year" (lit. "in year one"; Dan 7:1; Ezra 5:1)

Instrumental ("with," "through"): בְּחָכְמָה "through any wisdom" (Dan 2:30)

כְּ-

Comparative ("like," "as"): לְבוּשֵׁהּ כִּתְלַג חִוָּר "his garment was white as snow" (lit. "his garment, like snow [it was, namely] white"; Dan 7:9)

לְ-[34]

Temporal ("for a period of time"): לְעָלְמִין "forever" (Dan 2:4)

Relational ("with regard to"): הֵן תֶּהֱוֵא אַרְכָה לִשְׁלֵוְתָךְ "So that your prosperity may be prolonged" (lit. "so that there may be length to your prosperity"; Dan 4:24)

Directional ("to, toward, into"): אֱדַיִן דָּנִיֵּאל לְבַיְתֵהּ "then Daniel went to his home" (Dan 2:17); לְגוֹא־אַתּוּן "into the midst of a furnace" (Dan 3:6)

מִן

Spatial ("[away] from"): מִן־יְדָי "from my hands" (Dan 3:15)

Temporal ("since, from"): מִן־יוֹמָת עָלְמָא "from old days" (Ezra 4:15)

Comparative ("bigger, smaller, etc. than," "different from"): מְשַׁנְיָה מִן־כָּל־חֵיוָתָא "different from all the beasts" (Dan 7:7)

עַל

Spatial ("on, upon"): עַל־גִּירָא דִי־כְתַל "upon the plaster of the wall" (Dan 5:5); in a more idiomatic sense: מַלְכָּא שַׂגִּיא טְאֵב עֲלוֹהִי "the king was exceedingly glad" (lit. "the king—very good on him"; Dan 6:24)

Spatial[35] ("to, toward"): וּמַנְדְּעִי עֲלַי יְתוּב "and my reason returned to me" (Dan 4:31, 33)

Relational ("against"): עַל־שַׁדְרַךְ מֵישַׁךְ וַעֲבֵד נְגוֹ "against Shadrach, Meshach, and Abednego" (Dan 3:19)

קֳדָם

Spatial ("before"): עֲנוֹ כַשְׂדָּיֵא קֳדָם־מַלְכָּא "the Chaldeans answered before the king" (Dan 2:10); בֵּאדַיִן גֻּבְרַיָּא אִלֵּךְ הֵיתָיוּ קֳדָם מַלְכָּא "then these men were brought before the king" (Dan 3:13)

---

34. Note that the preposition לְ also serves as the marker of the direct (accusative) object (see the section on "Morphosyntax").

35. In BA עַל apparently took the place of BH אֶל ("to," "toward").

As in BH, prepositions can take suffixes, in which case the same pronominal suffixes apply that are also used for nouns: לֵה "to/for him," לִי "to/for me," בַּהּ "in it (f.)," בָּךְ "in you," etc. A particular use of בְּ is with a proleptic suffix: בַּהּ־שַׁעֲתָה "in that hour/when" (lit. "in it, the hour"), בֵּהּ־זִמְנָא "at that time" (lit. "in it, the time").

Note that in the cases of עַל and קֳדָם the pronominal suffixes for plural (!) nouns are used: עֲלָיִךְ "on/upon you"; עֲלוֹהִי "on/upon him"; קֳדָמַי "before me";[36] קֳדָמוֹהִי "before him."

PRONOUNS

Personal Pronouns

1 c. sg.	אֲנָה	"I"
2 m. sg.	אַנְתָּה	"you"
3 m. sg.	הוּא	"he"
3 f. sg.	הִיא	"she"
1 c. pl.	אֲנַחְנָא	"we"
2 m. pl.	אַנְתּוּן	"you (all)"
3 m. pl.	אִנּוּן, הִמּוֹ, הִמּוֹן	"they"
3 f. pl.	אִנִּין	"they"

Usually, the personal pronoun is used as the subject of a sentence or in order to emphasize the subject ("I, Daniel, saw the vision . . ."; Dan 8:15).

In the case of the 3 person pl., however, it can also assume the role of the (accusative) object:

יְהַב הִמּוֹ בְּיַד נְבוּכַדְנֶצַּר

"He gave *them* into the hand of Nebuchadnezzar" (Ezra 5:12)

---

36. In the case of קֳדָם + 1 sg. suf., the Masoretes added an accent (metheg) to the opening syllable in order to lengthen it, instead of reducing it to a half-vowel: קֳדָמַי instead of קְדָמַי.

As in BH, the pronouns of the third person serve as a copula (connector) between two nouns, expressed through the auxiliary verb "be" ("A *is* B" or "A *was* it"):[37]

אֲנַחְנָא הִמּוֹ עַבְדוֹהִי דִי־אֱלָהּ שְׁמַיָּא

"We *are* the servants of the God of heaven" (Ezra 5:11)

אֲמַרְנָא לְהֹם מַן־אִנּוּן שְׁמָהָת

"We asked them what their names *were*" (Ezra 5:4)

עֲנֵה מַלְכָּא וְאָמַר לְדָנִיֵּאל אַנְתָּה הוּא דָנִיֵּאל

"The king answered and said to Daniel: 'So you *are* Daniel . . .'" (Dan 5:13)

Demonstrative Pronouns ("this," "these/those")

The "these"-type pronouns indicate persons or things within close distance (the pronoun can be placed before or after the noun to which it refers).

m. sg.	דְּנָה
f. sg.	דָּא
c. pl.	אִלֵּן / אִלֵּין

Examples

עַל־רָזָה דְנָה "regarding this mystery" (Dan 2:18)

כָּל־אִלֵּין תַּדִּק וְתֵרֹעַ "It [the fourth kingdom] shall crush and shatter all these" (Dan 2:40)

The "those"-type pronouns indicate spatial and sometimes also emotional distance (the pronoun is usually placed after the noun to which it refers).

m. sg.	דִּכֵּן / דֵּךְ
f. sg.	דָּךְ
	דִּכֵּן
c. pl.	אִלֵּךְ

---

37. Cf. Dan 2:9, 20, 28, 38, 47; 3:15; 4:19, 27; 6:11; 7:17; Ezra 5:11, 13; 6:15.

Examples

הֵן קִרְיְתָא דָךְ תִּתְבְּנֵא   "If that city is rebuilt . . ."[38]
(Ezra 4:13, 16)

גֻּבְרַיָּא אִלֵּךְ לָא־שָׂמוּ עֲלָיִךְ מַלְכָּא טְעֵם   "Those men pay no heed to you, O
king" (Dan 3:12)

---

38. The speakers in this case are the opponents to the rebuilding of Jerusalem (Ezra 4:13).

The Verb

Biblical Aramaic has four verbal inflections: *perfect, imperfect, jussive*, and *imperative*. Since their consonantal forms have many similarities with BH, it is relatively easy to identify them, even though the respective vowel patterns are different.

As in all Semitic languages, the three root consonants (or *radicals*[39]) are associated structurally with a characteristic vowel pair for the perfect and imperfect. For example, the root כתב "write" has an *a/u* pair: *a* in the perfect and a *u* in the imperfect: יִכְתֻּב/כְּתַב; שׁאל "ask, request" has an *a* in both perfect and imperfect; יִשְׁאַל/שְׁאֵל; יכל "be able to" has an *e* in the perfect and an *u* in the imperfect: יִכֻּל/יְכֵל. It is not important to know these vowel pairs for each root; one should, however, be aware that different verbs follow different patterns.

The following paradigms show the basic structure of each of the four inflections. As in BH, the individual forms consist of prefixes and suffixes added to the three radicals. Note that in order to recognize a form as perfect, imperfect, jussive, or imperative it is helpful to develop a sense of what the consonantal forms (without masoretic vowel points) look like. This is also important with regard to extrabiblical, unpointed texts.

THE PERFECT

Forms of the perfect[40] are composed of the verbal root plus personal endings. Only the 3 m. sg. has no ending.

---

39. From Latin *radix* "root."
40. Some textbooks refer to this as the "suffix conjugation."

Structure

3 m. sg.	כתב	3 m. pl.	כתב + וּ
3 f. sg.	כתב + ַ ת	3 f. pl.	כתבָ + וּ[41]
2 m. sg.	כתב + תָ / תְ	2 m. pl.	כתב + תוּן
2 f. sg.		2 f. pl.	
1 c. sg.	כתב + ֵ ת	1 c. pl.	כתב + נָא

Paradigm

3 m. sg.	כְּתַב[42]	3 m. pl.	כְּתַבוּ
3 f. sg.	כִּתְבַת	3 f. pl.	כְּתַבָ[43]
2 m. sg.	כְּתַבְתָּ / כְּתַבְתְּ	2 m. pl.	כְּתַבְתּוּן
2 f. sg.		2 f. pl.	
1 c. sg.	כִּתְבֵת	1 c. pl.	כְּתַבְנָא

Exercise 5: Perfect Forms (base conjugation)

Parse the following forms and translate them with the help of a dictionary.

שְׁלַחְנָא	כְּתַבוּ
אֲמַר	שְׁאֵל
קְצַף	שְׁלַחְתּוּן
שְׁמְעֵת	יְהַבְתְּ
נֶפְקַת	יְכֵלְתְּ

41. The masoretic Qere suggests a reading הָ-; the Ketib, however, indicates that the feminine ending was not distinct from the masculine ending.

42. Note that the same vowel pattern is used for some of the nouns (m. sg. abs.): דְּהַב "gold," תְּלַג "snow."

43. Cf. footnote 41.

מְלַחְנָא	סְלֵקַת
נְפַלוּ	סְלֵקוּ

THE IMPERFECT

Due to their characteristic prefixes, imperfect[44] forms are easy to identify. As in BH, the forms of the 3 f. sg. and 2 m. sg. are identical. The plural forms, however, differ from BH: the 3 and 2 m. pl. have a final ן-; also, unlike BH, there is a distinct form for the 3 f. pl.

Structure

3 m. sg.	י + כתב	3 m. pl.	י + כתב + וּן
3 f. sg.	ת + כתב	3 f. pl.	י + כתב + ן
2 m. sg.	ת + כתב	2 m. pl.	ת + כתב + וּן
2 f. sg.		2 f. pl.	
1 c. sg.	א + כתב	1 c. pl.	נ + כתב

Paradigm

3 m. sg.	יִכְתֻּב	3 m. pl.	יִכְתְּבוּן
3 f. sg.	תִּכְתֻּב	3 f. pl.	יִכְתְּבָן
2 m. sg.	תִּכְתֻּב	2 m. pl.	תִּכְתְּבוּן
2 f. sg.		2 f. pl.	
1 c. sg.	אֶכְתֻּב	1 c. pl.	נִכְתֻּב

A special imperfect form is used for the root הוה "to be." Instead of the regular י prefix, it has ל: לֶהֱוֵה "he/it will be."

וְעִם־חֵיוַת בָּרָא לֶהֱוֵה מְדֹרָךְ

"And with the animals of the field *will be* your dwelling" (Dan 4:22)

---

44. Some textbooks refer to this as the "prefix conjugation."

וְהַכְרִזוּ עֲלוֹהִי דִּי־לֶהֱוֵא שַׁלִּיט תַּלְתָּא בְּמַלְכוּתָא

"And they made a proclamation concerning him [Daniel], that *he should rank* third in the kingdom" (Dan 5:29)

Exercise 6: Imperfect Forms (base conjugation)

Parse the following forms and translate with the help of a dictionary.

יִשְׁכְּנָן		יִשְׁלַט	
יִסְגֻּד		תַּעַבְדוּן	
תִּרְשֻׁם		יֵאמַר	
תֶּעְדֵּא		אֶקְרֵא	
יַחְלְפוּן		נֵאמַר	

THE IMPERATIVE

Since the imperative occurs only in direct speech, it is usually easy to recognize. However, the consonants of the m. sg. and pl. forms are identical with those of the 3 m. sg. and 3 m. pl. pf.

Structure

m. sg.	כתב	m. pl.	כתב + ו
f. sg.	כתב + י	f. pl.	

Paradigm

m. sg.	כְּתֻב	m. pl.	כְּתֻבוּ
f. sg.	כְּתֻבִי	f. pl.	

Exercise 7: Imperative Forms (base conjugation)

Parse the following forms and translate with the help of a dictionary.

שְׁבֻקוּ	פְּרֻק
אֱמַר[45]	אֲכֻלִי
אֱמַרוּ[46]	אֱזֵל

THE JUSSIVE

The jussive is a command form of the third person (e.g., "let him/her/them perish"). In most cases, the jussive form is identical with the imperfect. The difference lies in the stress patterns: whereas the imperfect has the emphasis on the last syllable (*yaktúb*), the jussive carries it on the first (*yáktub*). A clear distinction can be drawn in the plural forms, where the imperfect ends in וֹן, which is omitted in the corresponding jussive forms:

יֵאבַדוּ "Let them perish"; the imperfect in this case would be יֵאבְדוּן "they will perish." אַל־יִשְׁתַּנּוֹ "Do not let it [your face, pl.] change"; impf. יִשְׁתַּנּוֹן.[47]

As usually in BH, the jussive has אַל as a negative particle, whereas the imperfect has לָא; cf. אַל־יְבַהֲלָךְ "let it not terrify you."

While the jussive is a command form of the third person, jussive forms can also occur in the second person, replacing the imperative. This is the general rule with prohibitions. Since the imperative cannot be negated, the jussive takes its place: אַל־תְּהוֹבֵד "do not destroy."

As in the imperfect, the jussive of הֲוָה has a ל prefix: לֶהֱוֵא "let him/it be," e.g., יְדִיעַ לֶהֱוֵא "let it be known."[48]

---

45. Note that the perfect 3 m. sg. is אֲמַר.
46. Compare the perfect 3 m. pl.: אֲמַרוּ.
47. Note, however, that the 3 f. pl. seems to keep the final וֹן also in the jussive: לֶהֶוְיָן; as the context of Dan 5:17 suggests, this is a jussive rather than imperfect form: "Let them [your gifts] be for yourself."
48. יְדִיעַ is a Peᶜil ptc. of ידע (see under "conjugations" below).

THE CONJUGATIONS

Like most other Semitic languages, BA distinguishes among three different *modes of action*:

1. The *basic* mode (in grammar books also referred to as Pe‛al or, borrowing from BH, Qal, which lit. means "light/simple").

2. The *factitive-resultant* mode. Some textbooks refer to this category as "intensive action," the assumption being that its main characteristic—the doubled second radical—indicates that originally the verb was repeated (*katab katab* > *katteb*) in order to "intensify" its meaning. Other studies have argued, however, that the doubling expresses the *result* or *facticity* of (repeated) action. Note that, according to masoretic rules, the second consonant cannot be doubled if it is א, ה, ח, ע, or ר. However, this is a secondary rule that, in all likelihood, does not reflect the spoken Aramaic behind the biblical texts. For the purpose of clarity, the charts below double the second radical of the paradigm verb פעל ("to do") in all three conjugations of the factitive-resultant group (Pa‛‛el, Pa‛‛al, and Hitpa‛‛al).

3. The *causative* mode. Semitic languages regard certain kinds of action (such as "show" or "bring") as the *result of a cause* (to *make* someone *see* something = to *show*; to *make* something *go* = to *bring*).

These three different modes of action can be correlated with three different *modes of speech*: active, passive, and reflexive. This simply means that the same fact or event can be accentuated in different ways: "The teacher introduced a new student"; "A new student was introduced by the teacher"; "The student introduced herself."

If one combines the three modes of action with the three modes of speech, the result is a system of nine distinct conjugations. The seven conjugations of BH fall into this system as follows:

BH

	base conjugation	factitive-resultant	causative
Active	Qal (or Pa‛al)	Pi‛‛el	Hip‛il
Passive	Nip‛al	Pu‛‛al	Hop‛al
reflexive-passive	Nip‛al	Hitpa‛‛el	

One notices that only the factitive-resultant group has three distinct conjugations for active, passive, and reflexive. In the causative group, a reflexive conjugation is missing. The base group has not retained its original passive or reflexive conjugations. Here the Nip‛al (an originally independent conjugation) is used instead.

BA

	base conjugation	factitive-resultant	causative
active	Peᶜal (Qal)	Paᶜᶜel	Hapᶜel (ʾApᶜel)
passive	Peᶜil	Paᶜᶜal (only ptc.)	Hopᶜal, Hapᶜal (only ptc.)
passive-reflexive	Hitpeᶜel (ʾItpeᶜel)	Hitpaᶜᶜal (ʾItpaᶜᶜal)	

The only empty position in the BA system is the passive-reflexive of the causative group. In comparison, BA shows three major differences from BH:

1. In the base family, there are passive and reflexive conjugations that are missing in BH; conversely, BA has not retained the Nipᶜal conjugation.
2. The passive form of the factitive-resultant group is not a Puᶜᶜal (as in BH) but a Paᶜᶜal, which is limited to the participle.
3. In the causative group, there are two passive forms: Hopᶜal (as in BH) and Hapᶜal (for participles).

Note that, alternatively to the -ה and -הת prefixes of the Hitpeᶜel, Hitpaᶜᶜal, and Hapᶜel, BA also uses -א and -את (ʾItpeᶜel, ʾItpaᶜᶜal, ʾApᶜel).[49]

A few verbs have a -שׁ prefix in the causative group. The causative active conjugation is then called *Šapᶜel* (instead of Hapᶜel) and the causative reflexive *Hištapᶜal*. There is general agreement that the -שׁ prefix is an Akkadianism, since one finds the שׁ-causative (instead of the ה-causative) also in Babylonian and Assyrian. Verbs with שׁ-causative include the following:

שֵׁיזִב	"deliver/free"[50]	*root:*	עזב
שֵׁיצָא	"fulfill"[51]	*root:*	יצא
שַׁכְלִל	"fulfill"	*root:*	כלל

Basic Verbal Patterns

Due to the very limited number of BA texts, many of the verbal paradigms are incomplete. Especially for the so-called weak verbs,[52] sometimes only a few examples are attested, mostly for the 3 m. sg./pl. and 2 m. sg./pl.

---

49. These -א and -את prefixes are not be confused with the -א prefix of the 1 sg. impf.
50. In some dictionaries listed as שׁיזב.
51. In some dictionaries listed as שׁיצא.
52. The term "weak" in this case refers to verbs that have one or more root consonants/radicals that can either drop, assimilate, or change into a different consonant.

The following charts give the full paradigm of the strong[53] verb for all the conjugations. Not all of these forms are attested (some only in extrabiblical sources).[54] Not included are the forms of the 2 f. sg./pl., which do not occur in BA and only scarcely in epigraphic texts of Imperial Aramaic.

Peʿal (basic active)

		perfect		imperfect		imperative
3 m. sg.		כְּתַב		יִכְתֻּב		
3 f. sg.		כִּתְבַת		תִּכְתֻּב		
2 m. sg.		כְּתַבְתְּ/כְּתַבְתָּ		תִּכְתֻּב		כְּתֻב (m.), כְּתֻבִי (f.)
1 c. sg.		כִּתְבֵת		אֶכְתֻּב		
3 m. pl.		כְּתַבוּ		יִכְתְּבוּן		
3 f. pl.		כְּתַבָן[55]		יִכְתְּבָן		
2 m. pl.		כְּתַבְתּוּן		תִּכְתְּבוּן		כְּתֻבוּ
1 c. pl.		כְּתַבְנָא		נִכְתֻּב		

Peʿil (basic passive)

The characteristic feature of this conjugation is the long /ī/, which is written with a *mater lectionis* in most, though not all, cases. There are no imperfect forms in the Peʿil.

		perfect
3 m. sg.		כְּתִיב
3 f. sg.		כְּתִיבַת
2 m. sg.		כְּתִיבְתָּ
1 c. sg.		כְּתִיבֵת
3 m. pl.		כְּתִיבוּ
3 f. pl.		כְּתִיבָן
2 m. pl.		כְּתִיבְתּוּן
1 c. pl.		כְּתִיבְנָא

---

53. "Strong" means that all root consonants remain stable throughout the paradigm.
54. The paradigms at the end of this book list all attested forms.
55. Cf. footnote 41.

Hitpeᶜel (basic reflexive)

In this conjugation a prefix הת- is added. It merges with the prefixes of the imperfect and the participle: מִתְכְּתֵב > מְהִתְכְּתֵב; יִתְכְּתֵב > יְהִתְכְּתֵב.

Note that in BA, as in BH, a metathesis (switch of consonants) occurs when the root begins with a sibilant (ז, צ, שׁ). Thus the Hitpeᶜel of שׁכח is הִשְׁתְּכַח (instead of הִתְשְׁכַח). Additionally, in the case of זמן the Hitpeᶜel prefix changes to הִזְדְּ-: הִזְדְּמַנְתּוּן (instead of הִתְזְמַנְתּוּן).

		perfect		**imperfect**		**imperative**
3 m. sg.		הִתְכְּתֵב		יִתְכְּתֵב		
3 f. sg.		הִתְכַּתְבַת		תִּתְכְּתֵב		
2 m. sg.		הִתְכְּתֵבְתָּ הִתְכְּתֵבְתְּ		תִּתְכְּתֵב		
1 c. sg.		הִתְכַּתְבֵת		אֶתְכְּתֵב		
3 m. pl.		הִתְכְּתִבוּ		יִתְכַּתְבוּן		
3 f. pl.		הִתְכְּתִבָה		יִתְכַּתְבָן		
2 m. pl.		הִתְכְּתֵבְתּוּן		תִּתְכַּתְבוּן		
1 c. pl.		הִתְכְּתֵבְנָא		נִתְכְּתֵב		

Paᶜᶜel (factitive-resultant active)

The Paᶜᶜel forms double the second radical. The vowel that precedes the doubled radical is *a* (*pataḥ*). Since the Paᶜᶜel does not require any additional prefixes (except for the ptc., מ-), its consonantal structure looks exactly like the Peᶜal.

Note that in cases where the second consonant is א, ה, ח, ע, or ר it cannot be doubled, according to masoretic rules. The preceding *a* (*pataḥ*) is then sometimes (although not always) lengthened to *ā* (*qāmeṣ*; substitutional lengthening): בָּרֵךְ "he blessed" (3 m. sg. pf., with lengthening) but יִמְחֵא "he will hinder" (3 m. sg. impf., without lengthening).

		perfect		imperfect		imperative
3 m. sg.		כְּתַב		יִכְתֻּב		
3 f. sg.		כִּתְבַת		תִּכְתֻּב		
2 m. sg.		כְּתַבְתְּ		תִּכְתֻּב		כְּתֻב
1 c. sg.		כִּתְבֵת		אֶכְתֻּב		
3 m. pl.		כְּתַבוּ		יִכְתְּבוּן		
3 f. pl.		כְּתַבָן[56]		יִכְתְּבָן		
2 m. pl.		כְּתַבְתּוּן		תִּכְתְּבוּן		כְּתֻבוּ
1 c. pl.		כְּתַבְנָא		נִכְתֻּב		

Hitpaᶜᶜal (factitive-resultant reflexive/passive)

The Hitpaᶜᶜal has a doubled second radical and, in addition, the prefix הת- that merges with the prefixes of the imperfect (יהת- > ית-). As with the Hitpeᶜel forms, a metathesis occurs in the imperfect when the first root consonant is a sibilant (שׂ, ז, or צ): יִצְטַבַּע (instead of יתְצַבַּע, with additional ת > ט shift).

		perfect		imperfect		imperative
3 m. sg.		הִתְכַּתַּב		יִתְכַּתַּב		
3 f. sg.		הִתְכַּתְּבַת		תִּתְכַּתַּב		
2 m. sg.		הִתְכַּתַּבְתְּ		תִּתְכַּתַּב		
1 c. sg.		הִתְכַּתְּבֵת		אֶתְכַּתַּב		
3 m. pl.		הִתְכַּתַּבוּ		יִתְכַּתְּבוּן		
3 f. pl.		הִתְכַּתַּבָן[57]		יִתְכַּתְּבָן		
2 m. pl.		הִתְכַּתַּבְתּוּן		תִּתְכַּתְּבוּן		
1 c. pl.		הִתְכַּתַּבְנָא		נִתְכַּתַּב		

56. Cf. footnote 41.
57. Cf. footnote 41.

Hap‘el/’Ap‘el (causative active)

The prefix -הַ (in some cases -אַ) is the characteristic element of this conjugation. Unlike BH, this prefix is also retained in some of the imperfect forms: יְהַשְׁפֵּל. The typical vowel pattern is *a–ē/ī*.

	perfect	imperfect	imperative
3 m. sg.	הַכְתֵּב	יַכְתֵּב or יְהַכְתֵּב	
3 f. sg.	הַכְתְּבַת	תַּכְתֵּב or תְּהַכְתֵּב	
2 m. sg.	הַכְתֵּבְתְּ	תַּכְתֵּב or תְּהַכְתֵּב	הַכְתֵּב
1 c. sg.	הַכְתְּבֵת	אַכְתֵּב or אֲהַכְתֵּב	
3 m. pl.	הַכְתִּבוּ	יַכְתְּבוּן or יְהַכְתְּבוּן	
3 f. pl.	הַכְתִּבָו	יַכְתְּבָן or יְהַכְתְּבָן	
2 m. pl.	הַכְתֵּבְתּוּן	תְּהַכְתְּבוּן or תַּכְתְּבוּן	הַכְתִּבוּ
1 c. pl.	הַכְתֶּבְנָא	נַכְתֵּב or נְהַכְתֵּב	

Hop‘al (causative passive)

The Hop‘al has the -הָ prefix plus the characteristic vowel *o*.[58] There are no imperfect forms in the Hop‘al.

		perfect
3 m. sg.		הָכְתַּב
3 f. sg.		הָכְתְּבַת
2 m. sg.		הָכְתַּבְתָּ
1 c. sg.		הָכְתְּבֵת
3 m. pl.		הָכְתַּבוּ
3 f. pl.		הָכְתְּבָו
2 m. pl.		הָכְתַּבְתּוּן
1 c. pl.		הָכְתְּבְנָא

---

58. Short, open *o* as in "shock."

Exercise 8: Perfect Forms in Various Conjugations

Parse and translate the following forms.

קְטִילַת	הֻנְחַת
לָא בַּטִּלוּ	שַׁבַּחֵת
הַקְרִבוּ	שַׁבַּחְתָּ
אִתְיָעַטוּ[59]	הִשְׁתְּכַח
הִשְׁתְּכַחָנָה	הִתְנַדַּבוּ
כְּפִתוּ	הַזְדְּמִנְתּוּן[60]

Exercise 9: Imperfect Forms in Various Conjugations

Parse and translate the following forms.

יִתְעֲבֵד	תִּקְרַב
תְּהַנְזִק	תְּקַבְּלוּן
יַחְסְנוּן	יִתְיְהַבוּן
יְבַקַּר	יִשְׁתַּמְעוּן

59. Note that in BA, as in BH, the Masoretes do not double א, ה, ח, ע, and ר. In most cases, the preceding vowel is lengthened instead ("substitutional lengthening").

60. In addition to the ת/ז metathesis, the ת of the Hitpeʿel changes to ד.

THE PARTICIPLE

Since the participle is grammatically a noun, it has the endings of a noun in the absolute state. On its verbal side, the participle is included in the verbal stem system; as such, it can occur in the Peꜥal, Paꜥꜥel, Hapꜥel, and their related passive and reflexive conjugations.

Peꜥal

m. sg.	כְּתֵב	m. pl.	כָּתְבִין
m. pl.	כָּתְבָה[61]	f. pl.	כָּתְבָן

The Peꜥal participle has no characteristic prefix, which distinguishes it from participles of other conjugations; the characteristic vowel pattern is *ā–ē/ī*. Verbs with א, ה, ח, ע, or ר as the third consonant of the root have *ā–a*. Since this is the only instance of an *ā* in the opening syllable of a verb, it is a reliable sign of the Peꜥal participle.

קָטֵל	"the one who kills," "killing"
דָּלֵק	"burning"
אָמַר	"speaking" (sg.)
אָמְרִין	"speaking" (pl.)

Peꜥil

m. sg.	כְּתִיב	m. pl.	כְּתִיבִין
f. sg.	כְּתִיבָה	f. pl.	כְּתִיבָן

The passive participle has the same vowel pattern as the passive perfect (3 m. sg.): *ě–î* (in both cases, *î* serves as a marker for passive forms).

דְּחִיל	"being frightened" (m.)
דְּחִילָה	"being frightened" (f.)

In all of the following conjugations the participle has a ־מ prefix and the characteristic vowel pattern of the respective conjugation.

---

61. The participle vowel *ā*- is never reduced to -*ŏ*: כָּתְבָה *kātĕbâ* (not *kotbâ*), כָּתְבִין *kātĕbîn* (not *kotbîn*). The Masoretes indicate this by placing an accent (metheg) next to the *qāmeṣ*.

Hitpe‘el/Itpe‘el

m. sg.	מִתְכְּתֵב	m. pl.	מִתְכַּתְבִין
f. sg.	מִתְכַּתְבָה	f. pl.	

מִתְיְהֵב (used in the phrase לֶהֱוֵא מִתְיְהֵב "let it be given," Ezra 6:9)

Pa‘‘el

m. sg.	מְכַתֵּב	m. pl.	מְכַתְּבִין
f. sg.	מְכַתְּבָה	f. pl.	מְכַתְּבָן

מְהַלֵּךְ ("walking about")

Pa‘‘al (Pa‘‘el passive)

Although no passive perfect is attested in the Pa‘‘el, there is a passive participle. Unfortunately, it is only the literary context that suggests a passive meaning, since morphologically these forms could also be active (Pa‘‘el).[62]

m. sg.	מְכַתַּב	Pm. pl.	מְכַתְּבִין
f. sg.	מְכַתְּבָה	f. pl.	מְכַתְּבָן

מְבָרַךְ	"blessed"
מְכַפְּתִין	"bound" (m. pl. abs.; from the context of Dan 3:23–24 a passive meaning is clearly intended)
מְסַתְּרָתָא	"the hidden (things)" (f. pl. det.; from the context of Dan 2:22 a passive meaning is intended)

Hitpa‘‘al

m. sg.	מִתְכַּתַּב	m. pl.	מִתְכַּתְּבִין
f. sg.	מִתְכַּתְּבָה	f. pl.	

מִתְחַנַּן	"seeking mercy"
מִשְׂתַּכַּל	"considering" (root שׂכל)[63]

62. Only the m. sg. ptc. has a form that is morphologically distinct from the Pa‘‘el. However, all the pertinent verbs have a middle radical ר (מְבָרַךְ, מְעָרַב, מְפָרַשׁ), which can take a *pataḥ* in both the Pa‘‘el and Pa‘‘al. Thus it is the narrative context that decides whether a form should be analyzed as active (Pa‘‘el) or passive (Pa‘‘al): לֶהֱוֵא שְׁמֵהּ דִּי־אֱלָהָא מְבָרַךְ מִן־עָלְמָא וְעַד־עָלְמָא "Blessed be [rather than "blessing"] the name of God from age to age" (Dan 2:20).

63. Note that in BA, as in BH, there is a metathesis when the root begins with ז, שׂ, or צ.

Hapᶜel/ʾApᶜel

Note that, as with the imperfect forms, the Hapᶜel prefix ‑ה may or may not be written.

m. sg.	מְהַכְתֵּב or מַכְתֵּב	m. pl.	מְהַכְתְּבִין or מַכְתְּבִין
f. sg.	מְהַכְתְּבָה or מַכְתְּבָה	f. pl.	מְהַכְתְּבָן or מַכְתְּבָן

מַצְלְחִין	"prospering"
מַשְׁפִּיל	"putting down"[64]

Hapᶜal (Hapᶜel passive)

As in the Paᶜᶜel, there is also a passive participle in the Hapᶜel, although only one such form is attested in BA: מְהֵימַן (from the root אמן) "being faithful." Whereas the active participle has the pattern *mĕhaqtēl*, the passive participle has *mĕhaqtal*.

Exercise 10: Participle Forms in Various Conjugations

Parse and translate the following forms.

דָּלֵק	פָּלַח
רָפְסָה	מְמַלְלָה
סָגְדִין	מִתְעֲבֵד
מַצְלַח	מִתְנַשְּׂאָה
גְּמִיר	מְפָרַשׁ

---

64. As in other cases, the Hapᶜel might show an *î* instead of an *ê*.

THE INFINITIVE

In the Pe‘al, the infinitives absolute and construct have a מ-prefix (it is important not to confuse this with participle forms).[65] The vowel pattern is *i–a* (*miqtal*), with laryngeals involved also *a–a* or *e–a*.

Pe‘al infinitive
מִכְתַּב

מִכְנַשׁ   "to gather"

מֶעְבַּד   "to work"

In all other conjugations, the infinitive does not have a prefix; the characteristic vowel pattern is *ā–ā(h)* in the last two syllables. It is helpful to note that in most cases the infinitive is used with the preposition ל in order to indicate a final clause (as in BH), expressing purpose.

Hitpe‘el infinitive
הִתְכְּתָבָה

לְהִתְקְטָלָה   "in order to kill"

Pa‘‘el infinitive
כַּתָּבָה

קַטָּלָה   "to kill"

Hitpa‘‘al infinitive
הִתְכַּתָּבָה

הִתְנַדָּבָה   "to offer freely"

Hap‘el infinitive
הַכְתָּבָה

לְהַשְׁמָדָה וּלְהוֹבָדָה   "in order to destroy and blot out"

65. As a rule to memorize: in the Pe‘al the infinitive has a מ-prefix, whereas the participle does not. In all other conjugations it is the participle that has a מ-prefix, not the infinitive.

A distinct form for the *infinitive construct* is very rare in BA. Where it occurs, it has the vowel pattern *ā–û*.

הִתְנַדָּבוּת   "to offer freely" (hitpa. inf.)

לְהַצָּלוּתֵהּ   "in order to save him" (root: נצל, ha. inf. + 3 m. sg. suf.)

Exercise 11: Infinitive Forms in Various Conjugations

Identify the conjugation and translate the following forms.

מִבְעֵא	תַּקָּפָה
הִתְבְּהָלָה	הַשְׁכָּחָה
יַצָּבָא	מֶעְבַּד

Exercise 12: Mixed Verb Forms (I)

Parse and translate the following forms.

שָׁמְעִין	יִתְעֲבֵד
יִשְׁתַּמְּעוּן	מְכַפְּתִין
הָרְגִּשׁוּ וְהַשְׁכַּחוּ	מִתְכַּנְּשִׁין
מַחְצְפָה	מֵאמַר
יִשְׁפַּר	קְרָא
יִמְחֵא	פְּתִיחָן
יָכֵל לְשֵׁיזָבוּת	הֶחֱסַנוּ

מְשֵׁיזֵב	יַחְסְנוּן
תְּקִפַת	חַבְּלוּ
לְהִתְקְטָלָה	הֻשְׁפֵּלְתְּ

VERBS WITH SUFFIXES

Like nouns, verbs can carry pronominal suffixes. While suffixes attached to nouns are genitive objects, in combination with verbs they function as *accusatives* (or direct objects: "I see *you*," "He loved *her*").

Although the vowel structure changes when suffixes are added to verbs, it is relatively easy to identify the suffixes. Some of them are identical with the pronominal suffixes of nouns.

1 c. sg.	נִי־
2 m. sg.	־ךְ
3 m. sg.	־הֵ (after a consonant)
	־הִי (after a vowel)
3 f. sg.	־הַ
2 m. pl.	־כוֹן
1 c. pl.	־נָא

Examples

הַקְרִבוּהִי	"they approached *him*"
הוֹדַעְתֶּנָא	"you [sg.] let *us* know"
לָא חַבְּלוּנִי	"they did not hurt *me*"

However, for the 3 m. pl., the personal pronoun is used instead of a suffix:

וְהוֹתֵב הִמּוֹ בְּקִרְיָה דִּי שָׁמְרָיִן

"And he settled *them* in the city of Samaria" (Ezra 4:10)

וְלָא־בַטִּלוּ הִמּוֹ עַד־טַעְמָא לְדָרְיָוֶשׁ יְהָךְ

"And they did not stop *them* until a report reached Darius" (Ezra 5:5)

Imperfect Forms with Suffixes and Energic *Nun* (*-inn/-in*)

More frequently than in BH, Aramaic verb forms have an "energic *nun*" or *nun energicum* (n.e.). This means that an additional נ or a doubled נ (נּ) is placed between the verb and the suffix. Originally, this may have been done to give the verb a fuller sound and so to highlight it where it was considered the key element of a sentence. In BA, however, the energic *nun* does not seem to add any particular emphasis to the verb. It occurs in all instances of suffixed imperfect forms.

While the energic *nun* is largely insignificant for translation purposes, it is important to analyze it properly in order to avoid mistaking it for one of the root consonants:

יְשֵׁיזְבִנְכוֹן	"he can save you [pl.]"
יְהוֹדְעַנַּנִי	"they will let me know"

חֵלֶם חֲזֵית וִידַחֲלַנַּנִי וְהַרְהֹרִין עַל־מִשְׁכְּבִי וְחֶזְוֵי רֵאשִׁי יְבַהֲלֻנַּנִי

"I saw a dream *that scared me*, and thoughts on my bed and the visions of my head *troubled me*" (Dan 4:2)

Exercise 13: Verbs with Suffixes

Parse and translate the following forms.

לָא חַבְּלוּנִי	הַשְׁלְמַהּ
חַתְמַהּ	יִשְׁאֲלֶנְכוֹן
יְטַעֲמוּנֵהּ	יְבַהֲלֻנֵּהּ
הַשְׁלְטָךְ	הוֹדַעְתֶּנָא[66]

WEAK VERBS

The previous sections introduced the paradigm of the so-called strong verb, meaning that in all the forms, including the ones with suffixes, all three root consonants remain stable. The following paragraphs will focus on the weak verb. The term "weak" indicates that in some of their forms these verbs do not show the three radicals in the way that strong verbs do; one or more of their radicals either drop, assimilate, or change into a different consonant. If a root has two weak radicals (typically the first and the last), it is called "doubly weak."

The most common rules for weak verbs are the following:

1. Some verbs *drop* their initial consonant. Hence only the second and third consonants remain (e.g., הַב "give!" from יהב).
2. Some verbs *assimilate* their first or second consonants to what *follows or precedes* them (e.g., הַסִּקוּ "they brought up," 3 m. pl. ha. from סלק "to go up"). Assimilation occurs more extensively in BA than in BH, in which only the first consonant of certain verbs (like נתן "to give") assimilates to the one that follows it. Assimilation is typically expressed through a *dagesh forte* in the consonant to which the weak consonant assimilates.

66. ידע in the ha. "to let know/inform."

3. Some verbs *change* their first consonant if it is an א, ה, or י (e.g., הוֹדַע "he informed," 3 m. sg. ha. from ידע "to know").

4. Some verbs *change* their third consonant. This is the case primarily with verbs that have a final א or ה (e.g., צְבִית "I wanted," from צבא).

5. Special rules apply in cases where the middle radical of a verb is a vowel (*û* or *î*); see below under roots II *û/î* (or hollow roots).

In the following, these rules are applied to individual groups of weak verbs.

Roots Beginning with נ (I *n*)[67]

Two basic rules apply (as in BH):

1. The initial נ drops in the imperative: שֵׂא "take!" (from נשא); פֻּקוּ "go out!" (from נפק).

2. The נ can assimilate to the following consonant if there is no vowel between the two; in this case, the second radical is doubled: יִפֵּל (< ינפל) "he will fall" (נפל), יִתְּנִנַּהּ [68] (< ינתננה) "he gives it" (נתן). However, this rule is not as strict as in BH; in some cases נ remains unchanged: יִנְתְּנוּן "they will give."

Roots Beginning with י (I *y/w*)

The following phenomena occur in this group:

1. The intial י drops in the imperative: דַּע "know!" (ידע).

2. Among the I *y* roots is a group of verbs that were originally I *w*. In this case, the initial י turns into ו when a prefix is added and י becomes part of the opening syllable: הוֹדַע "he informed"[69] (ha.) (ידע, originally ודע); הוֹתֵב "he settled" (ha.) (יתב, originally ותב).

Roots Beginning with א (I ʾ)

In this group, the initial א disappears if it becomes part of the prefix syllable.

הֵימִן	"he trusted" (3 m. sg. ha. pf.) from אמן[70]	
לְמֵזֵא	"to heat" (pe. inf. + ל) from אזא	
לְמֵמַר	"as follows"[71] (cf. BH לֵאמֹר) from אמר	

(For אתה "go" and אבד "perish" see below.)

---

67. With regard to nomenclature, root consonants are numbered according to their position: I (first consonant), II (second consonant), III (last consonant). Thus I *n* (first consonant is a נ), II *ū* (the vowel *ū* in middle position), etc.

68. Imperfect form with n.e. and 3 f. sg. suf.

69. Originally *hawdaʿ* (> *hôdaʿ*).

70. The original form in this case was *haʾmen*. The opening syllable first dissimilated (*haymen*) and then contracted (*hēmin*).

71. However, the same form is written לְמֵאמַר in Dan 2:9.

Roots with a Long vowel in Middle Position (hollow roots; II *î/û*)

Instead of a consonant, hollow roots have an *î* or *û* in second position, which can change, depending on the form and conjugation of a given verb.

In the Pe‘al, the *î* and *û* are preserved (although not always written) in the imperfect, imperative, and infinitive, while they become *ā* or *a* in the perfect.

Imperfect: יְקוּם (קום) "he will rise"

Perfect: שָׂם "he placed" (שׂים); שַׂמְתָּ / שָׂמְתָּ "you placed"; בָּת "he spent the night" (בית); קָמוּ "they rose."

While these rules are essentially the same as in BH, the participles of hollow roots show some distinct forms in BA. In order to maintain the characteristic vowel pattern of the Pe‘al participle (*ā–e*), a consonant, א or י, is inserted instead of the long middle vowel. This gives the hollow root the appearance of a full three-consonantal form. From the root קום "stand up, rise," the following participles are attested:

קָאֵם (m. sg. abs.)

קָאֲמִין (Qere קָיְמִין) (m. pl. abs.)

קָאֲמַיָּא (m. pl. det.)

The same phenomenon of an inserted "artificial" consonant also occurs in the Pa‘‘el infinitive. Here too this was done to maintain the characteristics of the infinitive, the doubling of the middle radical and the *-a-ā(h)* vowel pattern: קַיָּמָה. However, since hollow roots technically do not have a second radical that could be doubled, other Pa‘‘el forms in Aramaic (and Hebrew) double the last consonant instead. This is then called *Polel* and, for the passive-reflexive category, *Hitpolel*. In BA, though, there is only one pertinent form, the 2 m. sg. pf. Hitpolel of רום: הִתְרוֹמַמְתָּ "you have exalted yourself" (Dan 5:23).

In the Hap‘el and Hop‘al forms, hollow roots typically shift the middle vowel for both II *û* and II *î* toward *î* or *ê*: הֲקֵים (ha.) "he raised"; הֳקִימַת (ho.) "it [the beast] was raised."

One finds somewhat unpredictable forms in the Pe‘il. The perfect has either *î* or *û*: שִׂים "he was put" (3 m. sg.); שֻׂמַת "it was placed" (3 f. sg.).

Roots Ending in י (III *y*)

Some of verbs with ה (or א) originally had י as their final radical, indicating that these roots ended in *-iy*.[72] This ending was preserved in a number of instances:

---

72. Because of the original *-iy* ending, the pertinent roots are classified here as III *y*, rather than III *h*.

1. In forms with personal endings or suffixes: חֲזַיְתָ "you have seen" (from חזה), צְבִית "I wanted" (from צבא), רְמֵינָא, "we cast" (from רמה).

2. The Peʿal pl. ptc. shows the form בָּנַיִן (from בנה; *bānyīn > bānayin*).

3. In the Hapʿel: הַגְלִי "he deported" (from גלה), הֶעְדִּיו "they took away" (from עדה).

In other cases, the original י contracted with vowels that preceded or followed it. The most frequent examples are:

1. 3 m. pl. pf. בְּנוֹ "they built" (*banayū > běnô*), עֲנוֹ "they answered" (from ענה).

2. 3 m. pl. impf. יִבְנוֹן "they will build" (*yibněyūn > yibnôn*).

אתא/אתה

The root אתה deserves particular mention, since it is one of the doubly weak verbs (Iʾ and III *y*). As such, both the final א/ה and the initial א can change. The attested forms are:

Perfect (pe.): אֲתָה "he came"; אֲתוֹ "they came"

Infinitive (pe.): לְמֵתֵא "in order to bring" (prep. ל + inf.; first consonant א is dropped)[73]

Participle (pe.): אָתֵה "coming"

Perfect (ha.): הַיְתִי "he brought," הַיְתִיו "they brought" (both initial and final consonants are י)

Infinitive (ha.): לְהַיְתָיָה "in order to bring" (prep. ל + inf.)

Perfect (ho.): הֵיתָיִת "it [f.] was brought"; הֵיתָיוּ "they were brought"

Roots with Identical Second and Third Consonants (geminate roots; II = III)

Roots with identical second and third consonants have two characteristics:

1. When there is no vowel between these consonants, the two merge into one.

    דָּקוּ   "they were shattered" (דקק; *daqqū > dāqû*)

    הֻעֲלוּ   "they were brought" (עלל ho.; *huʿalělû > huʿallû*)

73. See verbs Iʾ.

2. When there is no vowel between the first and second consonants, *regressive assimilation* occurs (the second consonant assimilates to the first).

הַדִּקוּ   "they broke in pieces" (דקק ha.; *hadqiqû > haddîqû*)

תַּדִּק   "it [f.] breaks in pieces" (דקק ha.; *tadqiq > taddiq*)

תַּדְּקִנַּה   "it breaks it in pieces" (דקק with n.e. and 3 f. sg. suf.)

עַל   "he entered" (עלל; *ʿelal > ʿal*)[74]

An Aramaic characteristic appears with the root עלל: In some cases nasalization or regressive assimilation dissolves when a נ, as a quasi-first consonant, is inserted.[75] The root seems to be נעל in these cases; thus it is important to know that this initial נ is a secondary feature.

הַנְעֵל   "he brought in" (עלל ha.; *haʿlel > haʿʿel > hanʿel*)

הַנְעָלָה   "to bring in" (עלל ha. inf.; *haʿlālâ > haʿʿālâ > hanʿālâ*)

Verbs with ח, ע, or ר

Verbs with ח, ע, or ר are not "weak" in the sense that these consonants drop, change, or assimilate. However, in a number of cases, the vowels associated with these consonants differ from the usual vowel patterns of verbs and participles.

A rule of thumb is that these laryngeals are preceded by *a* or *e* rather than *i/e* or *u/o*: אָמַר "saying," יָדַע "knowing" (whereas the pe. ptc. typically has an *ā–e* pattern, as in יָהֵב "giving"); הַצְלַח "he promoted" (whereas ha. pf. typically has *a–ē*, as in הַנְפֵּק "he came out"); יִסְבַּר "he intends" (whereas impf. typically has *u* rather than *a*).

Exercise 14: Weak Verbs

Parse, identify the root, and translate the following forms.

הַנְפֵּק		הֲקִימֶת	
שָׁרִיו		מַנִּיתָ	

---

74. Note that this form looks like the prep. עַל "above, on, over, to." In Dan 2:24 the verb and the preposition occur next to each other: דָּנִיֵּאל עַל עַל־אַרְיוֹךְ "Daniel went in to Arioch."
75. Cf. the discussion of ידע below.

אִתְכְּרִיַּת	בְּעֵינָא
הוֹדַע	נַדַּת
יִדְּרוּן	שָׂמֶת
תִּפְּלוּן	מַלִּל

SPECIAL VERBS

In most of the Semitic languages, certain consonants—especially נ (*nun*)—are assimilated to the *following* consonant when there is no vowel between the two consonants (יִנְתֵּן < יִתֵּן). This is called *progressive* assimilation. In BA there are also examples of *regressive* assimilation, meaning that a consonant—especially ל—is assimilated to the *preceding* consonant. This is the case with two very common verbs: הלך ("go, walk"; cf. BH) and סלק ("ascend, go up").

הלך "go"

Imperfect (pe.): יְהָךְ (< יְהֲלֵךְ) "it goes"

Infinitive (pe.): מְהָךְ "to go"

Note, however, that in forms with a vowel between ה and ל no assimilation takes place: מְהַלֵּךְ (pa. ptc.) "walking (back and forth)."

סלק "go up"

Perfect (ha.): הַסִּקוּ   "they took up"

Perfect (ho.): הֻסַּק   "he was taken up"

In the case of סלק another phenomenon occurs: in certain forms the assimilation of ל to ס triggers a *dissimilation*, in which ס splits into ס and נ. This results in a quasi three-consonantal form, נסק instead of סלק. This dissimilation occurs in the Hapʿel infinitive: הַנְסָקָה "to bring up"[76] (original הַסְלָקָה > assimilated הַסָּקָה > dissimilated הַנְסָקָה).

---

76. The full form in Dan 6:24 is לְהַנְסָקָה.

ידע "know"

ידע belongs to the I *y/w* verbs. In BH the imperfect is יֵדַע / יֵידַע with a long *ē*. Instead of this long vowel, BA inserts נ as an additional consonant (cf. סלק). Hence these forms look as if the root was נדע.

תִּנְדַּע	"you know"
אֶנְדַּע	"I know"
יִנְדְּעוּן	"they know"

הוה "be"

The imperfect prefix of the 3 m. sg. is ל (instead of the usual י):

וְעִם־חֵיוַת בָּרָא לֶהֱוֵה מְדֹרָךְ

"And with the animals of the field will be your dwelling" (Dan 4:22)

אבד "perish"

Like other roots of the I ʾ group, אבד ("perish"; ha. "destroy") can lose its initial א when a prefix is added. In BA אבד is attested mainly in the Hapʿel and Hopʿal, where א merges with the prefix syllables as follows: *haʾ-* > *hô-* (ha.) and *huʾ-* > *hû-* (ho.); in both cases ו replaces א.

תְּהוֹבֵד	"You will destroy" (2 m. sg. impf. ha.)
הוֹבָדָה	"To destroy" (inf. ha.)
הוּבַד	"He was destroyed" (3 m. sg. pf. ho.)

Note that ו is not part of the root but serves as a *mater lectionis* for *ô* in the Hapʿel and *û* in the Hopʿal.[77] It can also be written without a *mater*:

יְהֹבְדוּן	"They will destroy" (3 m. pl. impf. ha.)

---

77. In the ha. the original imperfect form was *těhaʾabed*, which developed into *těhābed* and finally *těhōbed*.

Exercise 15: Weak Verbs/Special Verbs with Suffixes

Parse and translate the following forms:

הֲתִיבוּנָא	בְּנָהִי
יִתְּנִנַּהּ	שְׁנוֹהִי
הַחֲוֻנִי	הוֹדַעְתַּנִי
יְחַוֻּנַּהּ	הַעֶלְנִי

Exercise 16: Mixed Forms (II)

Parse and translate the following forms:

תִּנְדַּע	יְהִיבַת
לִמְהָךְ	תְּדוּשִׁנַּהּ
סָלְקָן	יְהַעְדּוֹן
יְקוּמוּן	הֲקֵימֶת

הֲקִימַת	לְהוֹדָעָה
הֵיתָיוּ	הֲוֵית
שַׁנִּיו	הֲתִיבוּנָא
שָׁתֵה	לְהַשְׁנָיָה
סַתְרֵהּ	יִשְׁתַּנּוֹן
בְּנְיָתַהּ	הַנְעֵל

Syntax

MORPHOSYNTAX[78]

Genitive Chains

One of the most characteristic features that distinguishes Aramaic from its neighboring languages is its ways of constructing genitive (construct) chains. There are three types of genitive chains:

Type I

BA uses the same combination of noun (const. state) + genitive (det. state) that one also finds in BH.

> גּוֹא נוּרָא   "the middle of the fire" (Dan 3:25)

> גֹּב אַרְיָוָתָא   "the lions' den" (Dan 6:8, 13, 25)

To distinguish a determined from an undetermined genitive chain, the preposition ל is used (as in BH): מֶלֶךְ לְיִשְׂרָאֵל רַב "*a* great king of Israel." However, as the following examples show, the rules for genitive chains are not as strict as in BH:

> בַּר אֱלָהִין "*a* divine being" (lit. a "son of god"; Dan 3:25 [no ל in this case])

> פַּרְשֶׁגֶן אִגַּרְתָּא "*a* copy of the letter" (Ezra 4:11 [grammatically determined, although the context suggests that it should be undetermined])

---

78. Morphosyntax focuses on the relation between two linguistic units, which involves both morphological and syntactical features.

Type II

The most common way of expressing a genitive chain in BA is through a relative clause: גֻּבָּא דִּי אַרְיָוָתָא "the den, that of the lions" (Dan 6:17, 20). In this case, the noun in the construct state is replaced by the noun in the determinate state, followed by the relative particle דִּי.

Other examples:

מִלְּתָא דִּי־מַלְכָּה   "the word of the king" (lit. "the word, that of the king")

חֶזְוָא דִּי־לֵילְיָא   "the vision of the night"

שְׁבִיבָא דִּי נוּרָא   "the flame of the fire"

Type III

Yet a third possibility for genitive chains in BA is to add a possessive suffix to the first noun, followed by the relative particle:

שְׁמֵהּ דִּי־אֱלָהָא	"the name of God" (lit. "his name, that of God")
בְּיוֹמֵיהוֹן דִּי מַלְכַיָּא אִנּוּן	"in the days of these kings" (lit. "in their days, those of these kings")
עַבְדוֹהִי דִּי־אֱלָהּ שְׁמַיָּא וְאַרְעָא	"servants of the God of heaven and earth" (lit. "his servants, the ones of the God of heaven and earth")

Looking at the history of the Aramaic language, we see that this third option (especially in Syriac) becomes the standard syntagma.

Exercise 17: Genitive Chains

Translate the following genitive chains and indicate the type (I, II, III) to which they belong.

רוּחַ אֱלָהִין קַדִּישִׁין	מַלְכָּא דִּי בָבֶל
פְּשַׁר מִלְּתָא	מָאנַיָּא דִּי בֵית אֱלָהָא

חֶזְוֵי רֵאשִׁי	אֱלָהֲהוֹן דִּי־שַׁדְרַךְ מֵישַׁךְ וַעֲבֵד נְגוֹ
פִּסָּא דִּי־יְדָא	שָׁרְשׁוֹהִי דִּי אִילָנָא

The Particle of Existence אִיתַי / אִתַי

As in BH, in BA a special nominal particle, אִיתַי, indicates the existence of someone or something. This particle can carry pronominal suffixes (the same as are used for m. pl. nouns), in which case the following forms occur:

אִיתַי	"I am (there/available)"
אִיתַךְ	"you [sg.] are (there/available)"
אִיתוֹהִי	"he/it is (there)"
אִיתַינָא	"we are (there)"
אִיתֵיכוֹן	"you [pl.] are (there)"

בְּרַם אִיתַי אֱלָהּ בִּשְׁמַיָּא

"but there is a God in heaven" (Dan 2:28)

לָהֵן אֱלָהִין דִּי מְדָרְהוֹן עִם־בִּשְׂרָא לָא אִיתוֹהִי

"except the gods, whose dwelling is not with humankind" (lit. "except the gods, which *their dwelling* with the humans *it is not*"; Dan 2:11)

לֵאלָהָיִךְ לָא־אִיתַינָא פָּלְחִין

"we are not available to serve your gods" (lit. "as serving your gods"; Dan 3:18)

חֲלָק בַּעֲבַר נַהֲרָא לָא אִיתַי לָךְ

"you will have no possession in Abar Nahara"[79] (lit. "a possession in Abar Nahara will not be with you"; Ezra 4:16)

---

79. עֲבַר נַהֲרָא could be translated lit. "across the river" (cf. NRSV "the province Beyond the River"). However, since this was at the same time the official name of the province to which Judah/Jerusalem belonged, it is better to keep it as a proper noun: Abar Nahara.

The Accusative Particle יָת

Aramaic has an accusative particle, יָת (cf. Hebrew אֵת). However, this particle is more common in Old Aramaic inscriptions than in BA, where it occurs only once (with the suf. הוֹן-).

אִיתַי גֻּבְרִין יְהוּדָאִין דִּי־מַנִּיתָ יָתְהוֹן עַל־עֲבִידַת מְדִינַת בָּבֶל

"There are these Jewish men whom you have appointed over the affairs of the province of Babylon" (lit. "There are Jewish men that you have appointed *them* over the affairs[80] of the province of Babylon"; Dan 3:12)

ל as Accusative Particle

By far the most commmon way of introducing an accusative (direct) object is through the preposition ל, which functions in BA as an accusative particle. This may be confusing, since in BH ל typically introduces *dative* (indirect) objects, but only very rarely accusative objects.[81]

אֲמַר לְהוֹבָדָה לְכֹל חַכִּימֵי בָבֶל

"he commanded to kill *all the wise men* of Babylon" (Dan 2:12)

לָהֵן מִן־דִּי הַרְגִּזוּ אֲבָהֳתַנָא לֶאֱלָהּ שְׁמַיָּא

"because our fathers angered *the God of heaven*" (Ezra 5:12)

The Interrogative Particle ה

The interrogative particle ה precedes a word or phrase that introduces a question. It is vocalized either הַ *ha* or הֲ *hă*. Unlike English word order, the word order of an interrogative sentence in BA is the same as in that of an affirmative sentence. As such, ה serves as a question mark put before an affirmative/declarative clause.

אֱלָהָךְ דִּי אַנְתָּה פָּלַח־לֵהּ בִּתְדִירָא הַיְכִל לְשֵׁיזָבוּתָךְ מִן־אַרְיָוָתָא

"Has your God whom you serve continually been able to save you from the lions?" (closer to the original word order: "Your God, whom you serve continually, has he been able . . . ?"; Dan 6:21)

---

80. Grammatically singular.

81. Instances of ל as accusative marker typically occur in Late Biblical Hebrew and may be attributed to Aramaic influence.

הַצְדָּא לֵאלָהַי לָא אִיתֵיכוֹן פָּלְחִין

"Is it true that you are unwilling to worship my gods?" (lit. "Is it true—my gods you are not ready to worship?"; note the particle of existence אִיתֵיכוֹן; Dan 3:14)

The Particles מָה and מַן

The particle מָה "what?" introduces questions referring to objects; מַן "who?" refers to persons.

מַן־הוּא אֱלָה דִּי יְשֵׁיזְבִנְכוֹן מִן־יְדָי

"Who is the god who will deliver you from my hands?" (Dan 3:15)

וְלָא אִיתַי דִּי־יְמַחֵא בִידֵהּ וְיֵאמַר לֵהּ מָה עֲבַדְתְּ

"And there is no one who can restrain his hand or say to him 'What have you done?'" (Dan 4:32)

TENSES AND ASPECTS

The syntactical function of the tenses has been one of the most controversial issues in contemporary Semitic studies. Some have argued that the Semitic languages do not actually have "tenses"; their primary function is not to express *temporal* meaning but rather to distinguish between different *aspects* of action. Put in the most general terms, aspect theory does not categorize action according to past, present, and future but according to binary distinctions such as completed versus incomplete action, narrative versus descriptive, factual versus potential, or one-time event versus continuous activity. The main advantage of aspect theory is that it is more comprehensive than tense theory. For example, one of the main aspects of the perfect is "completed action." By definition, this pertains mostly to actions of the past; however, it is conceivable that something completed can also occur in the present or is envisioned to occur in the future.

While this discussion is ongoing, there is consensus that the relationship between tenses and aspects also depends on the genre of a given text (prose, narrative, poetry, prophecy, instruction, etc.). In the following, we will give a general description of the function of the perfect, participle, and imperfect, using both aspect and tense theory, then outline some of the specifics of the verbal syntax (impersonal speech and word order) of BA, and eventually turn to a syntactical analysis of narratives, which represent the main genre of BA texts.

The Perfect

The perfect is by far the most frequent tense in BA. This is due to the narrative character of the texts and to the fact that there is no "imperfect consecutive" or "*waw* imperfect" (*way-yiqtol*) in BA.

Probably the most basic characteristic of the perfect is that it expresses *completed action*. Apart from narrative contexts this pertains to three other areas:

1. *Performative speech*, in which the act of speaking coincides with the action that the speech announces:

עַל־דְּנָה שְׁלַחְנָא וְהוֹדַעְנָא לְמַלְכָּא

"Therefore, we *hereby send and inform* the king" (Ezra 4:14)

2. The *declarative perfect*, which is used in order to state or underline something that the speaker considers to be fundamentally true:

חָכְמְתָא וּגְבוּרְתָא יְהַבְתְּ לִי

"Wisdom and strength *you have (truly) given* me" (Dan 2:23)

3. The *future perfect*, in which the aspect of completion and certainty extends to events that are expected to occur in the future:

וּמַלְכוּתָה וְשָׁלְטָנָא וּרְבוּתָא דִּי מַלְכְוָת תְּחוֹת כָּל־שְׁמַיָּא

יְהִיבַת לְעַם קַדִּישֵׁי עֶלְיוֹנִין

"And the kingdom, the dominion, and the greatness of the kingdoms under the sky *will (indeed) be given* to the people of the saints of the Most High" (Dan 7:27)

The Participle

Although the participle is morphologically a noun, it plays an important role in the Aramaic tense system. It can be used for descriptive or illustrative purposes:

וְהוּא מְהַשְׁנֵא עִדָּנַיָּא וְזִמְנַיָּא מְהַעְדֵּה מַלְכִין וּמְהָקֵים

מַלְכִין יָהֵב חָכְמְתָא לְחַכִּימִין וּמַנְדְּעָא לְיָדְעֵי בִינָה

"And he is the one who changes times and seasons, deposes kings and sets up kings; he gives wisdom to the wise and knowledge to those who have understanding" (Dan 2:21)

כְּעַן אֲנָה נְבוּכַדְנֶצַּר מְשַׁבַּח וּמְרוֹמֵם וּמְהַדַּר לְמֶלֶךְ שְׁמַיָּא

"Now I, Nebuchadnezzar, worship, extol, and glorify the King of heaven" (Dan 4:34)

וּמִן־רְבוּתָא דִּי יְהַב־לֵהּ כֹּל עַמְמַיָּא אֻמַּיָּא וְלִשָּׁנַיָּא הֲווֹ זָאֲעִין וְדָחֲלִין מִן־קֳדָמוֹהִי

"And because of the greatness that was given to him, all nations, peoples, and tongues were standing in awe and fear of him" (Dan 5:19)

The participle is also chosen to emphasize habits, capabilities, or personal characteristics:

לָא חַכִּימִין אָשְׁפִין חַרְטֻמִּין גָּזְרִין יָכְלִין לְהַחֲוָיָה לְמַלְכָּא

"No wise man, magician, enchanter, or diviner is able to reveal [the mystery] to the king" (Dan 2:27)

The following examples show the difference between the participle and the perfect:

אִיתַי אֱלָהּ בִּשְׁמַיָּא גָּלֵא רָזִין וְהוֹדַע לְמַלְכָּא נְבוּכַדְנֶצַּר מָה דִּי לֶהֱוֵא בְּאַחֲרִית יוֹמַיָּא

"There is a God in heaven, who *is able to reveal* [ptc.] mysteries, and he *has disclosed* [pf.] to king Nebuchadnezzar what it is that will happen at the end of days" (Dan 2:28)

בֵּלְשַׁאצַּר מַלְכָּא עֲבַד לְחֶם רַב לְרַבְרְבָנוֹהִי אֲלַף וְלָקֳבֵל אַלְפָּא חַמְרָא שָׁתֵה

"King Belshazzar *made* [pf.] a great festival for his thousand lords, and before the thousand he *was drinking wine* [ptc.]" (Dan 5:1)

Participle and Perfect as a Combined Tense

In order to indicate an extended period of time in the past, BA combines the participle with the perfect (typically from הוה "to be"):

חָזֵה הֲוַיְתָ	"As you were looking . . ." (implied: "You were looking for a longer period of time," referring to Nebuchadnezzar's dream in Dan 2)
חָזֵה הֲוֵית	"As I was looking . . ." (in this case, "looking" refers to Daniel's entire vision in Dan 7)

The emphasis on an extended period of time also applies to the central vision of Daniel 7:

עִם־עֲנָנֵי שְׁמַיָּא כְּבַר אֱנָשׁ אָתֵה הֲוָה

"With the clouds of heaven someone like a human being *was coming*"[82] (7:13)

The Phrase ענה ואמר

Direct speech in BA is frequently introduced by a phrase combining the roots ענה "answer" and אמר "speak." Sometimes both are participles: עָנֵה וְאָמַר "he answered and said"; in other cases, however, ענה appears in the perfect. The following examples occur in the same narrative context of Daniel 2:5–10:

עָנֵה מַלְכָּא וְאָמַר

"The king answered [ptc.] and said [ptc.]" (2:5)

עֲנוֹ תִנְיָנוּת וְאָמְרִין

"They answered [pf.] for the second time and said [ptc.]" (2:7)

עֲנוֹ כַשְׂדָּאֵי קֳדָם־מַלְכָּא וְאָמְרִין

"The Chaldeans spoke [pf.] before the king and said [ptc.]" (2:10)

Participle and Imperative as a Combined Tense

Combining the imperative with the participle seems to suggest that something should be done (or avoided) *permanently*: וּזְהִירִין הֱוֹו "Be warned!" (Ezra 4:22); רַחִיקִין הֱוֹו "Stay away!" (Ezra 6:6)

The Imperfect

Whereas the perfect expresses completed action, the characteristic of the imperfect is that it is used for *incomplete action*. As such, one finds it regularly as a present and future tense.

עִשְׂבָּא כְתוֹרִין לָךְ יְטַעֲמוּן וְשִׁבְעָה עִדָּנִין יַחְלְפוּן עֲלָיךְ

"Grass *you will be made to eat* just like oxen, and seven ages *will pass* over you" (Dan 4:29)

---

82. בַּר אֱנָשׁ lit. translates as "a son of man." In contrast to New Testament usage, the phrase does not carry the connotation of a messianic title; in Dan 7:13 it is used in a descriptive manner: after a series of beasts that have *some* human characteristics ("reason," "eyes," etc.), it is finally a *fully* human being that takes dominion over the world of nations. בַּר in the sense of "one of" also occurs in Dan 3:25: בַּר־אֱלָהִין "one of the gods/a divine being."

However, the imperfect can also express the past *when following a perfect*. In this case, the imperfect explains, unfolds, or amplifies the main line of action:

חֵלֶם חֲזֵית וִידַחֲלִנַּנִי וְהַרְהֹרִין עַל־מִשְׁכְּבִי וְחֶזְוֵי רֵאשִׁי יְבַהֲלֻנַּנִי

"I *saw* [pf.] a dream and *it scared me* [impf.], and thoughts on my bed and the visions of my head *confused me* [impf.]" (Dan 4:2)

Besides action, the imperfect is also used to express intentions, inclinations, and wishes:

וִיהַבוּ גֶשְׁמֵיהוֹן דִּי לָא־יִפְלְחוּן וְלָא־יִסְגְּדוּן לְכָל־אֱלָהּ לָהֵן לֵאלָהֲהוֹן

"And they *gave* [pf.] their bodies because *they did not want to worship and bow* to any god except their own God" (Dan 3:28)

IMPERSONAL SPEECH

Impersonal speech, in which the subject of a sentence remains unspecific ("one should be more aware of the needs of others"; "they don't make cookies like these anymore," etc.), occurs quite frequently in BA texts. There are essentially two ways of expressing impersonal speech: the plural participle and third masculine forms (sg. and pl., pf. and impf.).

Examples of the participle in impersonal speech:

וְלָךְ טָרְדִין מִן־אֲנָשָׁא

"And they will drive you away from humans" (lit. "And you, driving away from humans"; Dan 4:22)

לָךְ אָמְרִין "To you someone said . . ." or "To you it is spoken . . ." (the participle here serves as an impersonal predicate; lit. "To you saying . . .'"; Dan 4:28)

Examples of the 3 m. sg./pl. in impersonal speech:

שְׁפַר קֳדָם דָּרְיָוֶשׁ "It pleased Darius" (lit. "It was pleasant before Darius"; Dan 6:2)

לִבְבֵהּ מִן־אֲנוֹשָׁא יְשַׁנּוֹן "His heart shall be changed from that of a human" (lit. "His heart they will change from that of a human"; Dan 4:13)[83]

---

83. In some translations also interpreted as jussive ("let them change," etc.); however, the grammatical form is a regular imperfect, instead of the "short" form (יְשַׁנּוּ) that one would expect for the jussive.

Exercise 18: Impersonal Speech

Translate the following sentences.

1. וִיקָרָה הֶעְדִּיו מִנֵּהּ

2. וְכָרוֹזָא קָרֵא בְחָיִל לְכוֹן אָמְרִין עַמְמַיָּא אֻמַּיָּא וְלִשָּׁנַיָּא

3. אָתַיָּא וְתִמְהַיָּא דִּי עֲבַד עִמִּי אֱלָהָא עִלָּיָא שְׁפַר קָדָמַי לְהַחֲוָיָה

4. וַאֲרוּ עִם־עֲנָנֵי שְׁמַיָּא כְּבַר אֱנָשׁ אָתֵה הֲוָה

וְעַד־עַתִּיק יוֹמַיָּא מְטָה וּקְדָמוֹהִי הַקְרְבוּהִי

WORD ORDER

Word order in Aramaic is relatively flexible. In particular, predicate and subject do not always necessarily follow one another, but sometimes form a bracket around a sentence. Hence it is not advisable to translate sentences from beginning to end, but rather to identify the predicate and subject first.

רוּחַ יַתִּירָה וּמַנְדַּע וְשָׂכְלְתָנוּ מְפַשַּׁר חֶלְמִין וַאַחֲוָיַת אֲחִידָן וּמְשָׁרֵא קִטְרִין הִשְׁתְּכַחַת בֵּהּ

The subject of this sentence is רוּחַ (in first position), the predicate הִשְׁתְּכַחַת (in penultimate position). The middle part of the sentence seems to add, parenthetically, what the excellent spirit enables Daniel to do: "An excellent spirit—knowledge, insight, (the ability to) interpret dreams, explain mysteries, and solve riddles—was found in him" (Dan 5:12).

There is, however, a marked tendency in BA to place the element that is considered the main subject (or topic) of a sentence in first position, although this may not be the *grammatical* subject or predicate.

וְלָךְ טָרְדִין מִן־אֲנָשָׁא

"And they will drive *you* away from humans" (lit. "And *you,* driving away from humans"; Dan 4:22)

לֵאלָהָא דִּי־נִשְׁמְתָךְ בִּידֵהּ וְכָל־אֹרְחָתָךְ לֵהּ לָא הַדַּרְתָּ

"*The God* in whose hand is your breath and all your ways are his [in his command] you have not honored" (Dan 5:23)

הוּא צַלְמָא רֵאשֵׁהּ דִּי־דְהַב טָב

"*This image*, its head was of fine gold" (Dan 2:32)

רָזָה דִּי־מַלְכָּא שָׁאֵל לָא חַכִּימִין אָשְׁפִין חַרְטֻמִּין גָּזְרִין יָכְלִין לְהַחֲוָיָה לְמַלְכָּא

"The riddle that the king asks—no wise man, magician, enchanter, or diviner is capable of disclosing [it] to the king" (Dan 2:27)

אָתוֹהִי כְּמָה רַבְרְבִין וְתִמְהוֹהִי כְּמָה תַקִּיפִין

"How great are his signs and how mighty are his wonders!" (lit. "His signs—how great they are! His wonders—how mighty they are!"; Dan 3:33)

וְכָל־רָז לָא־אָנֵס לָךְ

"And no riddle can baffle you" (lit. "and any riddle—it does not baffle you"; Dan 4:6)

A certain element can be placed at the beginning of a sentence in order to emphasize it.

וַאֲנָה לָא בְחָכְמָה דִּי־אִיתַי בִּי מִן־כָּל־חַיַּיָּא רָזָא דְנָה גֱּלִי לִי

"*But as for me*, it is not because I have more wisdom than any other living being that this mystery has been revealed to me" (Dan 2:30)

(Note that אֲנָה, although in initial position, is not the subject of this sentence, which is רָזָא "secret," and the predicate is גֱּלִי "has been revealed.")

אֲנָה דָנִיֵּאל שַׂגִּיא רַעְיוֹנַי יְבַהֲלֻנַּנִי וְזִיוַי יִשְׁתַּנּוֹן עֲלַי

"*As for me*, Daniel, my thoughts terrified me, and my face turned pale" (Dan 7:28)

וּשְׁאָר חֵיוָתָא הֶעְדִּיו שָׁלְטָנְהוֹן

"*Concerning the rest of the beasts*, their dominion was taken away"[84] (Dan 7:12)

---

84. Note that this is also a case of impersonal speech (the "beasts" are not the grammatical subject); lit. "Concerning the rest of the beasts, *they* took away their dominion."

Exercise 19: Word Order

Translate the following sentences and comment on the position of the verb, subject, and object.

1. מַלְכְּתָא לָקֳבֵל מִלֵּי מַלְכָּא וְרַבְרְבָנוֹהִי לְבֵית מִשְׁתְּיָא עַלַּלת

2. וּבַיְתָה דְּנָה סְתֵרֵהּ וְעַמָּה הַגְלִי לְבָבֶל

3. גֻּבְרַיָּא אִלֵּךְ לָא־שָׂמוּ עֲלַיִךְ מַלְכָּא טְעֵם

   לֵאלָהָיִךְ לָא פָלְחִין

   וּלְצֶלֶם דַּהֲבָא דִּי הֲקֵימְתָּ לָא סָגְדִין

4. אַנְתְּה מַלְכָּא רַעְיוֹנָךְ עַל־מִשְׁכְּבָךְ

   סְלִקוּ מָה דִּי לֶהֱוֵא אַחֲרֵי דְנָה וְגָלֵא רָזַיָּא הוֹדְעָךְ מָה־דִּי לֶהֱוֵא

   וַאֲנָה לָא בְחָכְמָה דִּי־אִיתַי בִּי מִן־כָּל־חַיַּיָּא רָזָא דְנָה גֱּלִי לִי

NARRATIVE SYNTAX

Unlike BH, BA does not have any consecutive tenses. There is, in particular, no *imperfect consecutive* (*waw* imperfect).[85] Consequently, the perfect and, to a lesser extent, the participle assume the role of the narrative past tense. In addition, the temporal particle אֱדַיִן "then" is often used to emphasize the progress of action.[86]

Coming from BH, one expects the predicate of narrative sentences to occur in the first or second position of the sentence. While this can be so in BA, the predicate quite frequently moves toward the end of a sentence.

אֱדַיִן לְדָנִיֵּאל בְּחֶזְוָא דִי־לֵילְיָא רָזָה גֱּלִי

"Then to Daniel in a vision of the night the mystery was revealed" (Dan 2:19a)

אֱדַיִן דָּנִיֵּאל בָּרִךְ לֶאֱלָהּ שְׁמַיָּא

"Then Daniel blessed the God of heaven" (2:19b)

---

85. However, much of the recent scholarly debate revolves around the question of whether Aramaic, at some point in its history, had a "*waw* imperfect," which then disappeared in Imperial Aramaic. One of the pertinent texts in this regard is the inscription of King Zakkur from Hamat (see appendix 1).

86. In BH the progress of action is expressed through the -ו of the *waw* imperfect.

Perfect and Participle as Narrative Tenses

As mentioned above, the perfect and the participle have specific functions in the tense system of BA. With regard to the narrative structure of a text, both forms can be used without significant difference in meaning. The story of Belshazzar's feast illustrates this feature well (Dan 5:1–10):

¹בֵּלְשַׁאצַּר מַלְכָּא עֲבַד לְחֶם רַב

Belshazzar the king *made* a great banquet.

²בֵּלְשַׁאצַּר אֲמַר בִּטְעֵם חַמְרָא

Belshazzar *said*, under the influence of the wine. . . .

³בֵּאדַיִן הַיְתִיו מָאנֵי דַהֲבָא

Then they *brought* the golden vessels. . . .

⁴אִשְׁתִּיו חַמְרָא וְשַׁבַּחוּ לֵאלָהֵי דַהֲבָא וְכַסְפָּא

They *drank* wine and *toasted* (to) the gods of gold and silver. . . .

⁵בַּהּ־שַׁעֲתָה נְפַקוּ אֶצְבְּעָן דִּי יַד־אֱנָשׁ וְכָתְבָן

In that moment the fingers of a human hand *appeared* and *wrote*. . . .

⁶אֱדַיִן מַלְכָּא זִיוֹהִי שְׁנוֹהִי

Then the king *turned* pale. . . .

⁷קָרֵא מַלְכָּא בְּחַיִל לְהֶעָלָה לְאָשְׁפַיָּא

The king *cried out* loudly to assemble the magicians.

⁸אֱדַיִן עָלְלִין כֹּל חַכִּימֵי מַלְכָּא

Then all the sages of the king *came*. . . .

⁹אֱדַיִן מַלְכָּא בֵּלְשַׁאצַּר שַׂגִּיא מִתְבָּהַל

Then King Belshazzar *became* greatly *terrified*.

¹⁰מַלְכְּתָא לָקֳבֵל מִלֵּי מַלְכָּא וְרַבְרְבָנוֹהִי לְבֵית מִשְׁתְּיָא עַלַּת

The queen, because of the words of the king and his officers, *went* into the banquet hall.

In vv. 1–6 and 10 the perfect assumes the role of the narrative tense (with the exception of כָּתְבָן in v. 5), whereas in vv. 7–9 it is a participle in that role. There does not seem to be any significant difference with regard to the syntactical function of the two. Note that for the verb עלל both perfect and participle forms are attested (vv. 8 and 10) without discernible difference in meaning.

Circumstantial Clauses

In BA a narrative typically consists of two basic components: the description of the action itself and the circumstances that illustrate, explain, or counteract the main plot. In both BA and BH different types of sentences (verbal and nominal) and the use of tenses indicate the difference between these two components of a narrative. A circumstantial clause can be, for example, a *nominative clause* (Dan 7:1):

בִּשְׁנַת חֲדָה לְבֵאלְשַׁצַּר מֶלֶךְ בָּבֶל דָּנִיֵּאל חֵלֶם חֲזָה

Action: "In the first year of Belshazzar, the king of Babylon, Daniel saw/had a dream"

וְחֶזְוֵי רֵאשֵׁהּ עַל־מִשְׁכְּבֵהּ

Circumstance: "and the visions of his head [happened when he was lying] on his bed."[87]

בֵּאדַיִן חֶלְמָא כְתַב רֵאשׁ מִלִּין אֲמַר

Action: "Then he wrote down the dream, (and) he told the sum of the matter."

Changing Word Order between Predicate and Subject

If circumstances themselves involve some kind of action, the difference from the main plot may be indicated through inverted word order of the predicate and subject (Dan 6:19):

אֱדַיִן אֲזַל מַלְכָּא לְהֵיכְלֵהּ וּבָת טְוָת

"Then the king went to his palace and spent the night fasting"

(*predicate—subject; action*)

---

87. In other words: "The visions happened when he was asleep." Translations tend to connect "dream" and "the visions of the head"; compare, e.g., NRSV: "Daniel had a dream and visions of his head as he lay in bed." This, however, does not match the imagery. As Dan 4:10 and 7:2, 7 suggest, Daniel does not see a vision, but he sees something *in* a vision. The idea seems to be that the prophet, while he is asleep, enters the realm of visions in which he then becomes privy to seeing specific images or events.

וְדַחֲוָן לָא־הַנְעֵל קָדָמוֹהִי

"and no diversion (?) was brought to him"

(*subject—predicate; circumstance*)

וְשִׁנְתֵּהּ נַדַּת עֲלוֹהִי

"and his sleep fled from him"

(*subject—predicate; circumstance*)

אֱדַיִן clearly indicates the progress of action: the king turns in for the night. The following sentences (with inverted word order) describe how he spent the night: fasting and sleepless, since he had given permission to throw Daniel in the lions' den.

ANALYTIC AND SYNTHETIC SYNTAX

Contemporary linguistics distinguishes between analytic and synthetic types of syntactic relationships of elements of a sentence. The following example may illustrate the difference:

The child

in the garden　　　　　　　*saw a bird*

These words can be used to create two different sentences:

The child in the garden saw a bird.

The child saw a bird in the garden.

In this case, it is the word order alone that determines the concrete meaning; the grammatical forms of the words in each sentence are exactly the same. Thus the difference in meaning occurs at the synthetic level of the sentence ("syn-thetic" meaning the way in which things are "put together").

The same difference in meaning can be achieved by introducing additional *analytic* elements, such as relative particles:

The child *who* was in the garden saw a bird.

The child saw a bird *that* was in the garden.

Instead of "analytic" one might also say "explicit" (vis-à-vis "implicit"/synthetic). Conjunctions, relative particles, prepositions, and so on fall under this rubric.

The use and the combination of synthetic and analytic tools are significant characteristics of any language. However, in contrast to the analytic elements, which most of the time are easy to recognize, the synthetic level of a language poses more of a challenge to the interpreter. This is particularly true for languages that we know only from a rather limited number of texts, such as BA.

ANALYTIC ELEMENTS

The Particle דִּי

דִּי has essentially three functions. It introduces:

1. relative clauses ("the woman *who* . . ."; "the flower *that* . . .")
2. object clauses ("you mentioned *that* . . ." ; "it is a law *that* . . .")
3. purpose clauses ("it was done *so that* . . .")

The use of דִּי as a relative pronoun (cf. BH אֲשֶׁר) is very common in BA, especially since it can be used to replace construct chains (see above). Sometimes a whole series of attributes can be added to a noun by using דִּי.

מָאנֵי בֵית־אֱלָהָא דִּי דַהֲבָה וְכַסְפָּא דִּי נְבוּכַדְנֶצַּר הַנְפֵּק מִן־הֵיכְלָא דִּי־בִירוּשְׁלֶם

"The vessels of the temple *that* are of gold and silver *that* Nebuchadnezzar had taken out of the temple, *which* is in Jerusalem" (Ezra 6:5)

וְכָל־דִּי לָא לֶהֱוֵא עָבֵד דָּתָא דִי־אֱלָהָךְ וְדָתָא דִּי מַלְכָּא

"Everyone *who* will not obey the law of your God" (lit. "the law, *that* of your God") and the law of the king" (lit. "the law, *that* of your king"; Ezra 7:26)

In some cases, דִּי expresses both the relative particle and the implied noun to which it refers ("the one who"/"that which"):

דִּי־הֲוָה צָבֵא הֲוָא קָטֵל וְדִי־הֲוָה צָבֵא הֲוָה מַחֵא וְדִי־הֲוָה

צָבֵא הֲוָה מָרִים וְדִי־הֲוָה צָבֵא הֲוָה מַשְׁפִּיל

"Whomever he wanted to kill he killed, and whomever he wanted to let live he let live; he raised up whomever he wanted, and he lowered whomever he wanted" (lit. "The one whom he wanted he killed; the one whom he wanted he let live; the one whom he wanted he raised up; the one whom he wanted he lowered"; Dan 5:19b)[88]

Exercise 20: The use of דִּי

Translate the following sentences and determine the function of דִּי.

1. וְדָנִיֵּאל עַל וּבְעָה מִן־מַלְכָּא דִּי זְמָן יִנְתֶּן־לֵהּ וּפִשְׁרָא לְהַחֲוָיָה לְמַלְכָּא

2. וּדְנָה כְתָבָא דִּי רְשִׁים מְנֵא מְנֵא תְּקֵל וּפַרְסִין

3. יְדִיעַ לֶהֱוֵא לְמַלְכָּא דִּי יְהוּדָיֵא דִּי סְלִקוּ מִן־לְוָתָךְ עֲלֶינָא אֲתוֹ לִירוּשְׁלֶם

4. כְּעַן מַלְכָּא תְּקִים אֱסָרָא וְתִרְשֻׁם כְּתָבָא דִּי לָא לְהַשְׁנָיָה כְּדָת־מָדַי וּפָרַס דִּי־לָא תֶעְדֵּא

5. וְאַף שְׁמָהָתְהֹם שְׁאֵלְנָא לְהֹם לְהוֹדָעוּתָךְ דִּי נִכְתֻּב שֻׁם־גֻּבְרַיָּא דִּי בְרָאשֵׁיהֹם

דִּי in Compound Conjunctions

Most of the BA conjunctions include דִּי. It is important to realize that each of these conjunctions has a wide range of possible meanings. The following are examples of the most typical uses of conjunctions with דִּי.

Temporal Clauses: כְּדִי

אֱדַיִן מַלְכָּא כְּדִי מִלְּתָא שְׁמַע שַׂגִּיא בְּאֵשׁ עֲלוֹהִי

"Then the king, *when* he had heard about the matter, great grief came upon him" (Dan 6:15)

Temporal/Final Clauses: עַד (דִּי)

עַד דִּי־תִנְדַּע דִּי־שַׁלִּיט עִלָּיָא בְּמַלְכוּת אֲנָשָׁא

"Until you have learned *that* the Most High is sovereign over the kingdom of humankind [= over a human kingdom]" (Dan 4:22)

Temporal/Causal Clauses: מִן דִּי

וְדִי אֲמַרוּ לְמִשְׁבַּק עִקַּר שָׁרְשׁוֹהִי דִּי אִילָנָא מַלְכוּתָךְ לָךְ קַיָּמָה מִן־דִּי תִנְדַּע דִּי שַׁלִּטִן שְׁמַיָּא

"And when they said to leave the stem of the tree and its roots [this means that] your kingdom will be yours [again], *when* you have come to acknowledge that Heaven is powerful" (Dan 4:23)

---

88. More common is דִּי in combination with מַה "what" or מַן "who": לְמַן דִּי יִצְבֵּא יְהָקֵים עֲלַהּ "Whomever he chooses he appoints over it [the kingdom of humans]" (Dan 5:21).

כָּל־קֳבֵל דְּנָה מִן־דִּי מִלַּת מַלְכָּא מַחְצְפָה וְאַתּוּנָא אֵזֵה יַתִּירָא

"Because of this, *because* the word of the king was [so] urgent and the oven was so overheated . . ." (Dan 3:22)

Causal Clauses: כָּל־קֳבֵל דִּי

אֱדַיִן דָּנִיֵּאל דְּנָה הֲוָא מִתְנַצַּח עַל־סָרְכַיָּא וַאֲחַשְׁדַּרְפְּנַיָּא כָּל־קֳבֵל דִּי רוּחַ יַתִּירָא בֵּהּ

"Then this Daniel distinguished himself above the officials and satraps *because* an excellent spirit was in him" (Dan 6:4)

כָּל־קֳבֵל דִּי מִן־קֳדָם מַלְכָּא וְשִׁבְעַת יָעֲטֹהִי שְׁלִיחַ לְבַקָּרָא עַל־יְהוּד וְלִירוּשְׁלֶם

"*For* [you] are sent by the king and his seven counselors to inquire about Judah and Jerusalem" (Ezra 7:14)

Adversative Clauses: כְּדִי / כָּל־קֳבֵל דִּי

לָא הַשְׁפֵּלְתְּ לִבְבָךְ כָּל־קֳבֵל דִּי כָל־דְּנָה יְדַעְתָּ

"You have not humbled your heart, *although* you knew all this" (Dan 5:22)

וְדָנִיֵּאל כְּדִי יְדַע דִּי־רְשִׁים כְּתָבָא עַל לְבַיְתֵהּ

"And Daniel—*although* he knew that the decree had been signed—went into his house" (Dan 6:11)

Purpose Clauses: עַל־דִּבְרַת דִּי

עַל־דִּבְרַת דִּי פִשְׁרָא לְמַלְכָּא יְהוֹדְעוּן

"*in order that* the interpretation may be known to the king" (Dan 2:30)

Other Conjunctions

הֵן ("if")

As in BH, הֵן introduces conditional clauses:

וְהֵן חֶלְמָא וּפִשְׁרֵהּ תְּהַחֲוֹן מַתְּנָן וּנְבִזְבָּה וִיקָר שַׂגִּיא תְּקַבְּלוּן

"But *if* you [can] tell me the dream and its meaning, then you shall collect/receive gifts, rewards, and great honor" (Dan 2:6)

Not every "if"-clause needs a main clause, if the consequence following from the "if"-clause appears to be obvious or self-evident:

הֵן אִיתֵיכוֹן עֲתִידִין דִּי בְעִדָּנָא דִּי־תִשְׁמְעוּן קָל קַרְנָא . . . תִּפְּלוּן וְתִסְגְּדוּן לְצַלְמָא דִּי־עַבְדֵת

וְהֵן לָא תִסְגְּדוּן בַּהּ־שַׁעֲתָה תִתְרְמוֹן לְגוֹא־אַתּוּן נוּרָא יָקִדְתָּא

"If you are there [and] ready that, at the time that you hear the sound of the horn, . . . you fall down and worship the statue that I have made, [*well and good*]. But if you do not worship, in the same hour you will be thrown into the middle of the fiery and burning oven." (Dan 3:15, lit.)

כָּל־קֳבֵל ("thus, therefore")

For causal relationships between main clauses and subordinate clauses כָּל־קֳבֵל is used. Note that כָּל־קֳבֵל, often in combination with דְּנָה, can also be used as a causal particle within a main clause. It may then be translated as "therefore," "accordingly," or "because of this":

כָּל־קֳבֵל דְּנָה מַלְכָּא דָּרְיָוֶשׁ רְשַׁם כְּתָבָא וֶאֱסָרָא

"Therefore King Darius signed the document and decree" (Dan 6:10)

כָּל־קֳבֵל דְּנָה מַלְכָּא בְּנַס

"Because of this the king was furious" (Dan 2:12)

Exercise 21: Conjunctions

Translate the following sentences.

1. וְדָנִיֵּאל כְּדִי יְדַע דִּי־רְשִׁים כְּתָבָא עַל לְבַיְתֵהּ

2. חָזֵה הֲוֵית עַד דִּי כָרְסָוָן רְמִיו וְעַתִּיק יוֹמִין יְתִב

3. יָדַע אֲנָה דִּי עִדָּנָא אַנְתּוּן זָבְנִין כָּל־קֳבֵל דִּי חֲזֵיתוֹן דִּי אַזְדָּא מִנִּי מִלְּתָא

4. לָהֵן מִן־דִּי הַרְגִּזוּ אֲבָהָתַנָא לֶאֱלָהּ שְׁמַיָּא יְהַב הִמּוֹ בְּיַד נְבוּכַדְנֶצַּר מֶלֶךְ־בָּבֶל

5. כְּעַן יְדִיעַ לֶהֱוֵא לְמַלְכָּא דִּי הֵן קִרְיְתָא דָךְ תִּתְבְּנֵא וְשׁוּרַיָּה יִשְׁתַּכְלְלוּן מִנְדָּה לָא יִנְתְּנוּן

6. כָּל־עַם אֻמָּה וְלִשָּׁן דִּי־יֵאמַר שָׁלוּ עַל אֱלָהֲהוֹן

דִּי־שַׁדְרַךְ מֵישַׁךְ וַעֲבֵד נְגוֹא הַדָּמִין יִתְעֲבֵד וּבַיְתֵהּ נְוָלִי

יִשְׁתַּוֵּה כָּל־קֳבֵל דִּי לָא אִיתַי אֱלָהּ אָחֳרָן דִּי־יִכֻּל לְהַצָּלָה כִּדְנָה

SYNTHETIC SYNTAX

Implicit Subjugation

Sometimes BA does not employ a conjunction to qualify the relationship between two sentences, but simply uses ו "and" as a connector, even though the sentence that the ו introduces functions as an adverbial clause. This is especially the case when consecutive meaning is intended ("and so"). However, there are also examples of object clauses and temporal clauses with ו:

שְׁפַר קֳדָם דָּרְיָוֶשׁ וַהֲקִים עַל־מַלְכוּתָא לַאֲחַשְׁדַּרְפְּנַיָּא מְאָה וְעֶשְׂרִין

"It pleased Darius *to set* 120 satraps over the kingdom" (lit. "It was pleasant before Darius, and he set over the kingdom . . ."; Dan 6:2)

יָהֲבִין לְהוֹן טַעְמָא וּמַלְכָּא לָא־לֶהֱוֵא נָזִק

"They [the satraps] reported to them *so that* the king would not suffer loss."

(lit. "They reported to them, and the king will not suffer loss"; Dan 6:3)

לָהֵן חֶלְמָא אֱמַרוּ לִי וְאִנְדַּע דִּי פִשְׁרֵהּ תְּהַחֲוֻנַּנִי

"Therefore, tell me the dream *so that* I know that you can [also] reveal its meaning to me" (lit. "Tell me the dream, and I will know . . ."; Dan 2:29)

A particularly intriguing case of implicit subjugation is Ezra 4:12b. Officials of the province of Samaria report to the Persian king that some of the Jews who had returned from Babylon had started to rebuild Jerusalem:

1. קִרְיְתָא מָרָדְתָּא וּבָאישְׁתָּא בָּנַיִן
2. וְשׁוּרַיָּא אֶשְׁכְלִלוּ
3. וְאֻשַּׁיָּא יַחִיטוּ

The first clause, using the participle (בָּנַיִן), indicates that the reconstruction of Jerusalem is underway. The second clause focuses on the completion of the city wall (אֶשְׁכְלִלוּ, pf.), whereas the third clause mentions repair work on the foundations, most likely those of the city walls (יַחִיטוּ, impf.). Most Bible translations interpret clauses 2 and 3, connected by ו, as two independent events. However, the order of events (the wall being finished before the foundations are repaired) seems awkward. Therefore, the perfect is best interpreted as anticipating a completed action in the future, whereas the imperfect indicates incomplete action in the present. As such, ו in clause 3 introduces an (implicit) temporal clause.

They are (re)building the city
and they will surely complete the walls,
once they have repaired the foundations.[89]

Implicit Attributive Clauses

In some cases ו is used instead of a relative pronoun to express attributive meaning:

חֵלֶם חֲזֵית וִידַחֲלִנַּנִי וְהַרְהֹרִין עַל־מִשְׁכְּבִי

"I saw a dream *that scared me*" (lit. "and it scared me") "and thoughts on my bed" (Dan 4:2)

וְדָנִיֵּאל עַל לְבַיְתֵהּ וְכַוִּין פְּתִיחָן לֵהּ בְּעִלִּיתֵהּ נֶגֶד יְרוּשְׁלֶם

"But Daniel went into his house, *which had* open windows in its upper chamber toward Jerusalem" (lit. "And Daniel went into his house; and open windows [were] to it in its upper chamber, facing Jerusalem"; Dan 6:11)

---

89. Ezra 4:13 lends further support to the interpretation that the completion of the wall is the main topic in this context: "Now let it be known to the king that, if this city is rebuilt and the walls finished, they will not pay tribute, custom, or toll."

Word List

Listed here are the most common verbs and nouns in BA that are worth memorizing. Among the particles, prepositions, and pronouns, only those are included that were not discussed in the grammar section of this textbook. Some of these words have equivalents in BH but are less common there or have slightly different meanings.

אַב	father
אבד	1. to perish (pe.) 2. to destroy, kill (ha.) 3. to be destroyed (ho.)
אִגְּרָה	letter
אֱדַיִן	then, after that
אָחֳרִי	another, a different one (f.)
אזל	to go, leave (pe.)
אָחֳרָן	another, a different one (m.)
אִילָן	tree
אכל	to eat (pe.)
אֱלָהּ	god, God
אֻמָּה	people, nation
אמר	1. to say (pe.) 2. to command (pe.)
אֱנָשׁ	human (being)

84

אֲרַע	land
אָשַׁף	magician, diviner
אתא / אתה	to come
אֲתַר	1. track 2. place
באש	to be evil
בהל	1. to frighten (pe.) 2. to do something in a hurry (hitpe.) 3. to be frightened/alarmed (hitpa.)
בטל	1. to stop, cease (pe.) 2. to make to stop, hamper (pa.)
בַּי / בַּיִת 90	house
בעא	1. to ask, request (pe.) 2. to seek (someone) (pa.)
בַּר	1. son 2. member of (expressing belonging)
ברך	to praise (pe. and pa.)
גְּבַר	1. man 2. a certain one
גּוֹ	midst, middle
גלא	to reveal
גְּשֵׁם	body
דְּהַב	gold
דור	to dwell
דחל	1. to fear (pe.) 2. to frighten (pa.)
דִּין	1. justice 2. judgment 3. court
דקק	to break into pieces (pe. and ha.)
דָּת	1. decree 2. law
הוא / הוה	1. to come to pass, happen (pe.) 2. to become (pe.)
הֵיכַל	1. palace (of the king) 2. temple

90. Although usually listed as בַּיִת, the absolute form of "house" in Aramaic is בַּי.

הלך	1. to come, go (pe.) 2. to walk about (pa. and ha.)
זִיו	1. complexion 2. splendor (of the face)
זְמָן	time
חבל	1. to destroy (pa.) 2. to be destroyed (hitpa.)
חַד	1. one (cardinal and ordinal number) 2. (x) times
חוא	1. to announce (pe.) 2. to show, interpret (pa. and ha.)
חזה	to see
חֵזוּ	1. vision 2. appearance
חַי	1. alive, living 2. life
חיא	1. to live (pe.) 2. to let live (ha.)
חֵיוָא	animal, beast
חַיִל	1. strength 2. army
חַכִּים	sage, wise man
חָכְמָה	knowledge, wisdom
חֵלֶם	dream
חֲסַף	clay, potsherd
חַרְטֹם	magician, astrologer
טעם	to feed (pa.)
טְעֵם	1. taste 2. decree 3. report 4. will, order
יַד	hand
ידע	1. to know (pe.) 2. to let know (ha.)
יהב	1. to bring, give (pe.) 2. to be given (hitpe.)
יְהוּדִי	Jew

יַצִּיב	certain, true (adj.)
יתב	1. to sit, dwell (pe.) 2. to cause to dwell (ha.)
כהל / יכל	to be able to
כֹּל	the whole, all
כנשׁ	to gather
כְּנָת	companion, associate
כְּסַף	silver
כְּעַן	(and) now
כַּשְׂדָּי	1. Chaldean 2. Chaldean as astrologer
כְּתָב	1. writing, inscription 2. decree, order
לִשָּׁן	tongue, language
מָאן	vessel
מְדִינָה	district, province
מטה	1. to reach (pe.) 2. to come upon (pe.)
מִלָּה	1. word 2. matter
מֶלֶךְ	king
מַלְכוּ	1. kingly power 2. kingdom 3. reign
מנה	1. to number, reckon (pe.) 2. to appoint (pa.)
מָרֵא	lord (a king, god)
נוּר	fire
נזק	1. to bother (pa.) 2. to cause trouble (ha.)
נפל	1. to fall, come down (pe.) 2. to fall down, bow to (pe.)
נפק	1. to come out (pe.) 2. to bring forth (ha.)
נתן	to give (pe.)
סגד	to worship, pay homage

סְלֵק	1. to ascend, come up (pe.) 2. to take up (ha.)
סָפַר	scribe
עֲבַד	to make, do, create, perform (pe.) to be made (hitpe.)
עִדָּן	1. time 2. year
עֲזַב	שֵׁיזִב to rescue, deliver (shapᶜel)
עֲלַל	1. to go in (pe.) 2. to bring in (ha.) 3. to be brought in (ho.)
עָלַם	eternity
עַם	nation, people
עֲנה	1. to answer (pe.) 2. to begin speaking (pe.)
פְּלַח	1. to revere (pe.) 2. to serve (pe.)
פֻּם	mouth
פַּרְזֶל	iron
פַּרְשֶׁגֶן	copy
פְּשַׁר	to interpret (pe. and pa.)
פְּשַׁר	interpretation
פִּתְגָּם	1. word, report 2. decree
צְבָא	to be inclined to do something, to be willing to (pe.)
צְלָא	to pray (pa.)
צְלֵם	1. image 2. idol
קַדִּישׁ	holy (adj.)
קוּם	1. to stand up, rise (pe.) 2. to stand (before) (pe.) 3. to announce, ratify (pa.) 4. to raise (ha.)
קְצָת	end, part
קְרָא	1. to call (pe.) 2. to read (pe.)

קְרֵב	1. to approach (pe.) 2. to offer (pa.) 3. to present, bring (before) (ha.)
רֵאשׁ	1. head 2. sum, essential
רוּחַ	1. wind 2. spirit (of God or a human)
רָז	secret, mystery
רמא	1. to throw, cast (pe.) 2. to be cast (hitpe.)
רַעְיוֹן	thought
רשׁם	to sign, inscribe
שַׂגִּיא	1. great 2. many, much
שִׂים	1. to put (pe.) 2. to be put (hitpe.)
שׁאל	1. to ask (pe.) 2. to request (pe.)
שְׁאָר	rest, remainder
שׁיזב	see עזב
שׁכח	1. to be found (hitpe.) 2. to find (ha.) 3. to receive (ha.)
שָׁלוּ	neglect, carelessness
שׁלח	to send (pe.)
שׁלט	to rule, have power (pe.)
שָׁלְטָן	1. dominion 2. realm
שְׁלָם	1. peace 2. well-being
שֵׁם	name
שְׁמַיִן	heaven
שׁמע	1. to hear (pe.) 2. to obey (hitpa.)
שׁנא	1. to change, become different (pe.) 2. to alter, cause to become different (pa.) 3. to change, to be changed (hitpa.)

שְׂרָא	1. to loosen (knots) 2. to abide (pe.) 3. to begin (pa.) 4. to become loose (hitpa.)
תּוּב	1. to return (pe.) 2. to restore (ha.)
תְּקַף	1. to grow strong, (negative) to harden (pe.) 2. to confirm (pa.)

Persian and Greek Loanwords

It is helpful to note a number of Persian and Greek loanwords in BA since, unlike Semitic words, these do not have a triconsonantal core with prefixes and suffixes.

PERSIAN

(Mostly administrative terminology; cf. Dan 3:2–3; 6:3–5)

אֲדַרְגָּזְרַיָּא	the advisers
אֲחַשְׁדַּרְפְּנַיָּא	the satraps
אֲפַרְסְכָיֵא	the prefects
גְּדָבְרַיָּא	the treasurers
דָּתָא	the law
הַדָּבְרַיָּא[91]	the state secretaries
הַדָּמִין	pieces
סָרְכַיָּא	the royal officials
פִּתְגָּמָא	the decree
תִּפְתָּיֵא	the police officers

---

91. Note that ה followed by a doubled consonant has nothing to do with the Hebrew article.

GREEK

(Musical instruments; cf. Dan 3:5–7)

סַבְּכָא	harp
סוּמְפֹּנְיָה	flute
פְּסַנְתֵּרִין	lyre
קִיתָרֹס	zither (guitar)

Comparative Word List (Aramaic/Hebrew)

Listed here are some of the most common Aramaic terms, which occur beyond BA in several Aramaic dialects, along with their Hebrew equivalents:

BA		BH
אֲזַל	"go," "leave"	אָזַל
אִנּוּן	"they" (m.)	הֵמָּה
אִנִּין	"they" (f.)	הֵנָּה
אֱנָשׁ	"human being"	אָדָם
אֹרַח	"way, path"	דֶּרֶךְ
בְּאִישׁ	"bad, evil" (adj.)	רַע
בְּעָה	"search, look for, request"	בִּקֵּשׁ
בַּר	"son"	בֵּן
גְּבַר	"man/a certain one"	אִישׁ
גַּו גּוֹא	"middle, midst"	תָּוֶךְ
גַּף	"wing"	כָּנָף
גְּשַׁם	"flesh, body"	בָּשָׂר
דוּר יְתַב	"sit (down), settle"	דּוּר יָשַׁב
דְּחַל	"fear, be afraid of"	יָרֵא
דִּי	"that, which" (relative particle)	אֲשֶׁר

93

דֵּךְ (m.) דָּךְ (f.) דִּכֵּן	"that one" (dem. pron.) "those" (c. pl.)	הַהוּא הַהִיא הָהֵם
דְּנָה (m.) דָּא (f.)	"this one" (dem. pron.)	זֶה זֹאת
הָא	"behold!"	הִנֵּה
הֵן	"if"	אִם
זְמָן	"time"	עֵת
חֲבַר	"friend, companion'"	רֵעַ
חֶדְוָה	"pleasure, joy"	שִׂמְחָה
חֲוָה	"tell, announce"	נָגַד
חֲזָה	"see"	רָאָה
טוּר	"mountain, rock"	הַר
יְקָר	"glory, honor"	כָּבוֹד
כְּהֵל יְכֵל	"be able to"	יָכֹל
כְּנַשׁ	"gather"	קָבַץ
כְּעַן כְּעֶנֶת	"(until) now"	עַתָּה
כָּרְסֵא	"throne"	כִּסֵּא
לָהֵן	"therefore, on this account"	עַל־כֵּן
מָאן	"vessel"	כְּלִי
מְזוֹן	"food, feed"	אֹכֶל
מִלָּה	"word, matter"	דָּבָר
נְפַק	"leave, go outside"	יָצָא
נְתַן יְהַב	"give"	נָתַן
עֲבַד	"do, make"	עָשָׂה
עֲדָה	"go, vanish"	סוּר
עֲלַל	"enter, go inside"	בּוֹא
שַׂגִּיא	"much, many"	מְאֹד

Idiomatic Expressions

Listed here are some of the idiomatic expressions in Daniel and Ezra whose meaning may be difficult to deduce from their literary contexts:

לָא־שָׂמוּ עֲלַיךְ טְעֵם

Lit. "They do not set on you thought"

Meaning: "They do not pay heed to you"[92] (Dan 3:12; 6:14)

וַאֲכַלוּ קַרְצֵיהוֹן

Lit. "And they ate their pieces" or "they ate them in pieces"

Meaning: "They [the Chaldeans] slandered them [the Jews]" (Dan 3:8)

יֵאמַר עַל

Lit. "He speaks against"

Meaning: "He says bad things about" (Dan 3:29)

כְּלָה

Lit. "As not"

Meaning: "As nothing" (Dan 4:32)

---

92. Note another idiom in which טְעֵם occurs: שִׂים טְעֵם "to set/issue a decree."

עַל דָּנִיֵּאל שָׂם בָּל לְשֵׁיזָבוּתֵהּ

Lit. "On Daniel he set [his] mind in order to save him"

Meaning: "He was determined to save Daniel" (Dan 6:15)

מַלְכָּא שַׂגִּיא טְאֵב עֲלוֹהִי

Lit. "The king, much good was on him"

Meaning: "The king was very glad" (Dan 6:24)

שְׁפַר קָדָמַי

Lit. "It is pleasant before me"

Meaning: "It pleases me" (Dan 3:32)

וְזִיוַי יִשְׁתַּנּוֹן עֲלַי

Lit. "And my splendor changed on me"

Meaning: "I [my complexion] turned pale" (Dan 4:33)

Note that BA frequently uses prepositions like עַל "on/upon" or קֳדָם "before" for idiomatic expressions, which may have to do with the fact that BA, in general, emphasizes spatial relations between agents or objects (e.g., נְהַר דִּי־נוּר נָגֵד וְנָפֵק מִן־קֳדָמוֹהִי "A river of fire issued and flowed out from before him," Dan 7:10).

מְלַח הֵיכְלָא מְלַחְנָא

Lit. "The salt of the palace we eat"

Meaning: "We are committed to the palace [= the king]" (Ezra 4:14)

מְשָׁרֵא קִטְרִין

Lit. "Someone who loosens knots"

Meaning: "Someone who solves problems" (Dan 5:12, 16)

קִטְרֵי חַרְצֵהּ מִשְׁתָּרַיִן

Lit. "The joints of his loins loosened" (Dan 5:6)

Meaning: The RSV and NRSV translate "his limbs gave way"; since these limbs are, however, located in the loin area, it seems likely that the actual meaning is along the lines of "he peed his pants."

לָא־שָׂמוּ עֲלַיִךְ מַלְכָּא טְעֵם

Lit. "They do not set [their ear?] on you, O king, [regarding the] decree."

Meaning: "They pay no heed to your decree, O king" (Dan 3:12; 6:14)

Appendix 1:
The Zakkur Inscription

One of the best-preserved Aramaic texts is the inscription of King Zakkur of Hamat (today's Afis in Syria) from the 8th century BCE. It represents the linguistic stage that preceded Imperial Aramaic. This inscription provides us with some important data about the development of the Aramaic language, especially with regard to Aramaic phonology and grammar. The following transcription includes most of stele I.[93]

(1) [מראה] נ[צ]בא זי שם זכר מלך חמת ולעש לאלור

(2) [א]נה זכר מלך חמת ולעש אש ענה אנה ו[חצל]

(3) נ[י] בעלשמין וקם עמי והמלכני בעלשמ[ין על]

(4) הזרך והוחד עלי ברהדד בר חזאל מלך ארם ש

(5) . . . . עשר מלכן [שת]

(9) . . . ושמו כל מלכיא אל מצר על הזר[ך]

(10) והרמו שר מן שר הזרך והעמקו חרץ מן חר[צה]

(11) ואשא ידי אל בעלש[מי]ן ויענני בעלשמי[ן וימל]

(12) [ל]ל בעלשמין אלי ביד חזין ו[ב]יד עדדן [ויאמר]

(13) [אלי] בעלשמין אל תזחל כי אנה המל[כתך ואנה א]

(14) [ק]ם עמך ואחצלך מן כל [מלכיא אל]

93. For the text of the entire inscription see H. Donner and W. Röllig, *Kanaanäische und aramäische Inschriften*, 3rd ed., 3 vols. (Wiesbaden: Harrassowitz, 1971), 1:37; 2:204–9; J. C. L. Gibson, *Textbook of Syrian Semitic Inscriptions*, vol. 2 (Oxford: Clarendon, 1975), 8–9.

General Comments

The inscription predates the shift from interdentals to dentals. In line 1 the relative pronoun is written זי (*dî*), not די, as in Imperial Aramaic; the same is the case in line 13: אל תזחל "Do not fear!" would be written אל תדחל in later Aramaic.

The inscription also shows that at this earlier stage in the development of the Aramaic script *matres lectionis* were used at the end of a word but not in the middle: "man" is written אש rather than איש, and the plural ending of masculine nouns (abs.) shows only the final ן without the additional י (ין-) (line 12: עדדן "prophets" instead of עדדין).[94]

Finally, the Zakkur inscription seems to use the *waw* imperfect (impf. consecutive) in line 11 ("and I lifted up," "and he answered me").[95]

Notes

(1) נצבא "the stele"; חמת "Hamat" and לעש "Luash" (place names); אלור "Iluwer" (divine name)

(2) ענה "humble" (adj.)

(4) הזרך "Ha<u>d</u>rak" (place name); הצלני pa. of הצל + 1 c. sg. suf. "he made me prosper"; הוחד ha. from יחד "to unify/make one, assemble"; ברהדד "Barhadad" and חזאל "Hazael": names of two Aramean kings who resided in Damascus

(9) אל dem. pron. "these" (cf. BH אלה)

(10) שר "wall"; חרץ "trench"

Translation

(1) (This is) the [s]tele that Zakkur, the king of [H]amat and Luash, erected for Iluwer [his lord]

(2) [I] am Zakkur, the king of Hamat and Luash. A humble man am I. Baalshamayin [made]

(3) me [prosper] and rose with me. And Baalshamayin made me king over

(4) Hadrak. Now Barhadad, the son of Hazael, the king of Aram, assembled against me

(5) sixteen kings. . . .

---

94. The name of the deity in this text has a dual-like ending (בעלשמין "Baalshamayin"), where the י is a full consonant; the same applies to the term חזין "seers," where the י belongs to the three-consonantal root and is thus fully pronounced (*ḥāziyīn*).

95. There has been extensive debate over whether these forms (and their equivalents in the Tel Dan inscription) should be regarded as *waw* imperfects (or consecutives). To get an impression of the different positions, see V. Sasson, "Some Observations on the Use and Original Purpose of the *Waw* Consecutive in Old Aramaic and Biblical Hebrew," *Vetus Testamentum* 47 (1997): 111–27; T. Muraoka and M. Rogland, "The *Waw* Consecutive in Old Aramaic? A Rejoinder to Victor Sasson," *Vetus Testamentum* 48 (1998): 99–104. In my translation I assume that pre–Imperial Aramaic did have the *waw* imperfect.

(9) . . . And all these kings laid siege to Hadr[ak].

(10) And they built a wall against the wall of Hadrak. And they dug a trench against its tr[ench].

(11) But I raised my hands to Baalsham[ay]in, and Baalshama[yin] answered me. And Baalshamayin [spoke]

(12) to me [thro]ugh seers and through prophets. And Baalshamayin [said

(13) to me]: "Do not fear, for I made you k[ing and I

(14) will ri]se with you. And I will make you prosper more than all [these kings]."

Appendix 2: Aramaic Samples from Qumran[96]

ABRAM'S PRAYER FOR GOD'S HELP[97]

(12) בליליא דן צלית ובעית ואתחננת ואמרת באתעצבא ודמעי נחתן בריך אנתה אל
עליון מרא כל

(13) עלמים די אנתה מרה ושליט על כולא ובכול מלכי ארעא אנתה שליט למעבד
בכולהון דין וכען

(14) קבלתך מרי על פרעו צען מלך מצרין די דברת אנתתי מני בתוקף עבד לי דין
מנה ואחזי ידך רבתא

(15) בה ובכול ביתה ואל ישלט בליליא דן לטמיא אנתתי מני וינדעוך מרי די אנתה
מרה לכול מלכי

(16) ארעה ובכית ושחית

Notes

(12) עצב hitp. "to be in distress"; ובעית צלית pa. of צלה; ובעית waw + pe. of בעה;
באתעצבא inf. hitpe. of עצב + prep. ב; דֶּמְעָה "tear"

(13) עלמים, apparently a Hebraic writing of עלמין

(14) פרעו צען קבל pe. "to lodge a complaint" (+ suf. "with somebody"); פרעו צען
"pharaoh of Zoan" (= Tanis, located in the Nile delta); די seems to serve as a
causal conjunction "because"; דברת 3 f. sg. pf. pe. of דבר "to lead away"; אנתתי
"my wife" (אַנְתָּה: "wife"); תּוֹקֶף "force"; BA would probably write אחזה

---

96. The Aramaic texts are quoted from the edition of K. Beyer, *Die aramäischen Texte
vom Toten Meer*, vol. 1 (Göttingen: Vandenhoeck & Ruprecht, 1984); the translations are mine.
Square brackets indicate a lacuna in the text.

97. Ibid., 175 (1QapGen XX,12–16).

(15) לטמיא inf. pa. of טמא.

(16) בכה "to cry"; חשא "to go silent"

Translation

(12) That night I prayed, pleaded, searched for mercy, and spoke in distress, while my tears kept running: "Blessed be you, eternal God, my Lord, forever

(13) and ever. You are Lord and have power over everything. And over all the kings of the world you are powerful to pronounce judgment on them. And now,

(14) I hereby lodge a complaint with you about the pharaoh of Zoan, king of Egypt, because my wife has been led away from me by force. Give me justice over him so that I will see your mighty hand

(15) upon him and his entire house. And let him not have power to dishonor my wife away from me.[98] So that they will know you, my Lord, that you are lord over all the kings of

(16) the world." And I cried and went silent.

LEVI'S FAREWELL SPEECH: A PRAISE OF WISDOM[99]

(3) ובש[נת מאה ותמנ]ה

(4) עשרה לחיי היא ש[את] די מית בה

(5) יוסף אחי קריתי לב[נ]י ו[לבניהון

(6) ושריתי לפקדה הנון כל ד[י] הווה

(7) עם לבבי עניח ואמרת לבני [שמעו]

(8) למאמר לוי אבוכון והציתו לפקודי

(9) ידיד אל אנה לכון מפקד בני ואנה

(10) קושטא לכון מהחוי חביבי ראש

(11) עובדיכון יהוי קושטא ועד

(12) עלמא יהוי קאים עמכון צדקה

. . . .

(15) . . . די זרע

(16) טאב טאב מהנעל ודי זרע ביש עלוהי תאיב זרעה

98. The phrase does not translate well into English. The idea is, however, that once the pharaoh had had intercourse with Sarah, she could no longer be Abraham's wife.

99. Beyer, *Aramäische Texte,* 205–7 (Cairo Geniza Testament of Levi, Cambridge Col. e, 3–16).

Notes

(4) מית = מות

(6) קריתי and שריתי are 1 c. sg. pf. (קרא/שרא) instead of BA קרית and שרית; הווה; cf. BA הֲוָו with additional *mater lectionis* ה-; לפקדה inf. pa. of פקד

(8) צות ha. "to listen/pay attention to"; פִּקּוּד "commandment" (פקד "to order, command")

(9) יַדִּיד "beloved"

(10) קוּשְׁטָא "truth"; מהחוי, in BA מהחוה, ptc. ha. of חוה; חַבִּיב "loved one"

(11) עוֹבָד "work"

(12) קאים, in BA קאם, ptc. pe. of קום (in combination with the jussive יהוי)

(15) זרע ptc. pe. (parallel to מהנעל as ptc. ha. of עלל)

(16) תוב ptc. of תאב, in BA תב; באיש, in BA ביש; תאיב, in BA תאב; טאב, in BA טב

Translation

(3) In the hundred and eigh-

(4) -teenth year of my life, the year when

(5) Joseph my brother died, I summoned my sons and their sons

(6) and began to tell them all the things that were

(7) on my heart. I spoke and said to my sons: "Listen

(8) to the speech of Levi, your father, and pay attention to the commandments

(9) of the beloved of God. I give you commandments, my sons, I

(10) introduce you to the truth, my beloved ones. The main subject

(11) of your deeds be truth, and

(12) always shall justice rise with you.

. . . .

(15) The one who sows

(16) good things harvests good things. But the one who sows bad things upon him returns his seed.

KING NABONIDUS'S PRAYER[100]

(1) מלי צל[ת]א די צלי נבני מלך בבל מלכא [רבא]

(2) בשחנא באישא בפתגם א[לה]א בתימן

(3) כתיש הוית שנין שבע ומן [די] שוי א[נגרי]

(4) וחטאי שבק לה גזר והוא יהודי ב[אדין]

(5) חו[י]ני וכתב למעבד יקר ור[ב]ו לשם א[לה]א כדי

---

100. Ibid., 223–24 (4QprNab).

(6) כתיש הוית בשחנא ב[אישא] בתימן

(7) שנין שבע מצלא הוי]ת קדם[אלהי כספא ודהבא

(8) אעא אבנא חספא מן די [אסב]ר די אלהין ה[מון]

Notes

(1) צלי, in BA usually spelled צלה; נְבְנַי Nebunay (Nabonidus)
(2) שְׁחֵן "ulcer"; תֵּימָן "Teman" (in southern Babylonia)
(3) כתש "strike"; מַן דִּי "the one who"; שוה pa. "determine"; אֲנַר "reward"
(8) חֲסַף "clay"; מַן דִּי "because" (conjunction); סבר pe. "think"

Translation

(1) The words of prayer that Nabonidus, the king of Babylon, the great king, prayed:

(2) "With an evil ulcer by the order of the God of Teman

(3) I was struck for seven years. But the one who determines my reward

(4) and my punishment saved himself a diviner, who was a Jew. And then this one

(5) informed me and wrote to give honor and veneration to the name of God. When

(6) I was struck with an evil ulcer in Teman

(7) for seven years, I (still) prayed before the gods of silver, gold,

(8) wood, stone, and clay because I thought they were gods."

Appendix 3: Two Sayings from the Wisdom of Ahiqar[101]

A caution against quick judgment:[102]

(1) ב[רי] אל ת[לו]ט יום

(2) עד תחזה [לי]לה

Note

(1) לוט pe. "to curse"

Translation

(1) My son, do not curse the day

(2) until you have seen the night.

---

101. Among the literary remnants of the Jewish military colony at Elephantine were fragments of texts featuring the sage Ahiqar. The texts include a narrative about Ahiqar at the court of the Assyrian kings Sennacherib and Esarhaddon and a collection of proverbs. Linguists nowadays agree that the narrative should be classified as Imperial Aramaic, whereas the proverbs show characteristics of a later stage (the so-called Western Aramaic family). Editions and translations of the texts are provided in A. Cowley, *Aramaic Papyri of the Fifth Century B.C.* (Oxford: Clarendon, 1923); J. M. Lindenberger, *The Aramaic Proverbs of Ahiqar* (Baltimore: Johns Hopkins University Press, 1983); and I. Kottsieper, *Die Sprache der Achiqarsprüche* (Berlin: de Gruyter, 1990).

102. Lindenberger, *Aramaic Proverbs*, 71.

A warning against loose speech:[103]

(1) ברי אל תאמר כל

(2) [זי] תאתה על לבך

(3) כזי בכל אתר [עיני]הם ואדניהם

(4) ל[הן] פמך אשתמר לך

(5) אל יהוה טרפי[ך]

Notes

(3) כזי introduces a causal clause ("because")

(4) להן "therefore"; פמך (noun פם) is direct object of אשתמר; אשתמר Itpeᶜel or ᵓItpeᶜal of שמר "watch over"; לך (*dativus ethicus*)[104] "for your own good"

(5) טרפין (abstract pl. of טרף) "grief"

Translation

(1) \<My son, do not utter everything\>
(2) [that] comes into your mind (heart),
(3) because in every place there are [eyes] and ears[105]
(4) There[fore], watch your mouth for your own good,
(5) do not let it become [your] grief.

---

103. Ibid., 73.
104. The "ethical dative" (usually the preposition ל plus suffix) indicates that a person, for their own good, ought to show an interest in or concern for a particular matter.
105. Lit. "their eyes and their ears."

Answers to Exercises

Exercise 1: Syllabic Structure of BA Words

מַלְכִין	"kings"	מַלְ ־ כִין (1. closed syllable, with silent *shewa*; 2. closed syllable)
כָּהֲנָא	"priest"	כָּ ־ הֲנָא (1. open syllable; 2. open syllable, with *ḥātēp pataḥ*)
שְׁמַיָּא	"heaven"	שְׁמַי ־ יָא (1. open syllable, with vocal *shewa*; 2. open syllable)
אַרְבְּעָה	"four"	אַרְ ־ בְּעָה (1. closed syllable, with silent *shewa*; 2. open syllable, with vocal *shewa*)
גַּלְגִּלּוֹהִי	"its wheels"	גַּלְ ־ גִּלְ ־ לוֹ ־ הִי (1. closed syllable, with silent *shewa*; 2. closed syllable; 3. open syllable; 4. open syllable)

הִתְנַבִּי	"he prophesied"	בִּי - נַב - הִתְ (1. closed syllable with silent *shewa*; 2. closed syllable; 3. open syllable)
יִתְרְמֵא	"he shall be cast"	רְמֵא - יִתְ (1. closed syllable, with silent *shewa*; 2. open syllable, with vocal *shewa*)
אַרְגְּוָנָא	"purple"	נָא - גְּוָ - אַרְ (1. closed syllable, with silent *shewa*; 2. open syllable, with vocal *shewa*; 3. open syllable)
לְהַשְׁכָּחָה	"in order to find"	חָה - כָּ - לְהַשְׁ (1. vocal and closed syllable, with vocal and silent *shewa*; 2. open syllable; 3. open syllable)

Exercise 2: Aramaic and Hebrew Word Comparisons

BA	BH		BA	BH	
שְׁלָם	שָׁלוֹם	"peace, well-being"	שְׁמַשׁ	שֶׁמֶשׁ	"sun"
זְרַע	זֶרַע	"seed"	תבר	שׁבר	"to break"
חֲדַת	חָדָשׁ	"new"	תּוֹר	שׁוֹר	"ox"
יעט	יעץ	"to advise"	תְּלַג	שֶׁלֶג	"snow"
צְלֵם	צֶלֶם	"statue, image"	כדב	כזב	"to lie"

Exercise 3: Basic Noun Parsings

שִׁמְשָׁא m. sg. det. "the sun"	יוֹמַיָּא m. pl. det. "the days"
מְדִינְתָּא f. sg. det. "the province"	חָכְמְתָא וּגְבוּרְתָּא f. sg. det. (2x) "wisdom and strength" (phrase)
נְבִזְבָּה f. sg. abs. "gift, present"	חֵיוָה f. sg. abs. "beast"
כָּהֲנַיָּא m. pl. det. "the priests"	שְׁאֶלְתָּא f. sg. det. "the request"
שָׁלְטָנָא m. sg. det. "the empire"	פַּחֲוָתָא f. pl. det. of the m. (!) noun פֶּחָה "governor"
תָּרְעַיָּא m. pl. det. "the gates"	שַׁעֲתָה f. sg. det. "the hour" (ה for א)
לִשָּׁנַיָּא m. pl. det. "the tongues, languages"	חֵיל שְׁמַיָּא m. sg. const. + m. pl. det. "the host of heaven"
עַרְוַת מַלְכָּא f. sg. const. + m. sg. det. "the dishonor of the king"	שִׁלְטֹנֵי מְדִינָתָא m. pl. const. + f. pl. det. "the officers of the provinces"

Exercise 4: Nouns with Suffixes

בְּרֵהּ m. sg. noun + 3 m. sg. suf. "his son"	אֲבָהָתִי m. pl. noun + 1 c. sg. suf. "my ancestors/fathers"
רָאשֵׁיהֹם m. pl. noun + 3 m. pl. suf. "their heads"	קַרְצֵיהוֹן m. pl. noun + 3 m. pl. suf. "their pieces"
שֵׁגְלָתֵהּ f. pl. noun + 3 m. sg. suf. "his wives"	גִּשְׁמַהּ m. sg. noun + 3 f. sg. suf. "its [the beast's] body"
לִבְבָךְ m. sg. noun + 2 m. sg. suf. "your heart"	בָּתֵּיכוֹן m. pl. noun + 2 m. pl. suf. "your houses"
מַעְבָדוֹהִי m. pl. noun + 3 m. sg. suf. "his works"	יְדָךְ m. sg. noun + 2 m. sg. suf. "your hand"
עֵינַי m. pl. noun + 1 c. sg. suf. "my eyes"	אַתְרֵהּ m. sg. noun + 3 m. sg. suf. "his [its] place"
נְבִזְבְּיָתָךְ f. pl. noun + 2 m. sg. suf. "your gifts"	שְׁמָהָתְהֹם m. pl. noun + 3 m. pl. suf. "their names"
מַלְכוּתֵהּ f. sg. noun + 3 m. sg. suf. "his kingdom"	עִלִּיתֵהּ f. sg. noun + 3 m. sg. suf. "its [the house's] upper chamber"

Exercise 5: Perfect Forms (base conjugation)

שְׁלַחְנָא	1 c. pl. "we sent"	כְּתַבוּ	3 m. pl. "they wrote"
אֲמַר	3 m. sg. "he said"	שְׁאֵל	3 m. sg. "he requested"
קְצַף	3 m. sg. "he was angry"	שְׁלַחְתּוּן	2 m. pl. "you sent"
שִׁמְעֵת	1 c. sg. "I heard"	יְהַבְתְּ	2 m. sg. "you gave"
נֶפְקַת	3 f. sg. "she came out"	יְכֵלְתָּ	2 m. sg. "you were able to"
מְלַחְנָא	1 c. pl. "we ate (the salt)"	סִלְקַת	3 f. sg. "she/it came up"
נְפַלוּ	3 f. pl. "they fell"	סְלִקוּ	3 m. pl. "they went up"

Exercise 6: Imperfect Forms (base conjugation)

יִשְׁכְּנָן	3 f. pl. "they will dwell"	יִשְׁלַט	3 m. sg. "he will rule"
יִסְגֻּד	3 m. sg. "he will bow to"	תַּעַבְדוּן	2 m. pl. "you will serve"
תִּרְשֻׁם	2 m. sg. "you will sign"[106]	יֵאמַר	3 m. sg. "he will say"
תֶּעְדֵּא	2 m. sg. "you will come"[107]	אֶקְרֵא	1 c. sg. "I will call"
יַחְלְפוּן	3 m. pl. "they will pass"	נֵאמַר	1 c. pl. "we will say"

---

106. It could also be 3 f. sg. "she will sign."
107. It could also be 3 f. sg. "she will come."

Exercise 7: Imperative Forms (base conjugation)

שְׁבֻקוּ	m. pl. "leave . . . in!"[108]	פְּרֻק	m. sg. "break!"
אֱמַר[109]	m. sg. "speak!	אֲכֻלִי	f. sg. "eat!"
אֱמַרוּ[110]	m. pl. "speak!"	אֱזֵל	m. sg. "go in!"

Exercise 8: Perfect Forms in Various Conjugations

קְטִילַת	3 f. sg. pf. pe. "she was killed"	הָנְחַת	3 m. sg. pf. ho. "he was deposed"
לָא בְטַלוּ	neg. particle + 3 m. pl. pf. pa. "they did not cease"	שַׁבְּחֵת	1 c. sg. pf. pa. "I worshiped"
הַקְרֻבוּ	3 m. pl. pf. ha. "they brought near"	שַׁבַּחְתָּ	2 m. sg. pf. pa. "you worshiped"
אִתְיָעַטוּ[111]	3 m. pl. pf. hitpa. "they counseled together"	הִשְׁתְּכַח	3 m. sg. pf. hitpe. "he was found"
הַשְׁכַּחְנָה	1 c. pl. pf. ha. "we found"	הִתְנַדַּבוּ	3 m. pl. pf. hitpa. "they gave freely"
כְּפִתוּ	3 m. pl. pf. Peꜥil "they were bound"	הִזְדְּמִנְתוּן[112]	2 m. pl. pf. hitpe. "you agreed together"

---

108. For the context cf. Dan 4:12.

109. Note that the 3 m. sg. pf. is אֲמַר.

110. Compare the 3 m. pl. pf.: אֲמַרוּ.

111. Note that, as in BH, א, ה, ח, ע, ר cannot be doubled in BA. In most cases the preceding vowel is lengthened instead.

112. In addition to the ת/ז metathesis, the ת of the Hitpeꜥel changes to ד.

Exercise 9: Imperfect Forms in Various Conjugations

יִתְעֲבֵד	3 m. sg. impf. hitpe. "he will be made"	תִּקְרֻב	3 f. sg./2 m. sg. impf. pa. "she/you will approach"
תְּהַנְזִק	3 f. sg./2 m. sg. impf. ha. "she/it will do damage"/"you will do damage"	תְּקַבְּלוּן	2 m. pl. impf. pa. "you will receive"
יַחְסְנוּן	3 m. pl. impf. ha. "they will possess"	יִתְיַהֲבוּן	3 m. pl. impf. hitpe. "they will give"
יְבַקַּר	3 m. sg. impf. pa. "he will inquire"	יִשְׁתַּמְּעוּן	3 m. pl. impf. hitpa. "they will obey"

Exercise 10: Participle Forms in Various Conjugations

דָּלִק	m. sg. abs. ptc. pe. "burning"	פָּלַח	m. sg. abs. ptc. pe. "serving"
רָפְסָה	f. sg. abs. ptc. pe. "trampling"	מְמַלְלָה	f. sg. abs. ptc. pa. "speaking"
סָגְדִין	m. pl. abs. ptc. pe. "worshiping"	מִתְעֲבֵד	m. sg. abs. ptc. hitpe. "making, doing"
מַצְלַח	m. sg. abs. ptc. ha. "prospering"	מִתְנַשְּׂאָה	f. sg. abs. ptc. hitpa. "carrying"
גְּמִיר	m. sg. abs. ptc. Peᶜil "completed"	מְפָרַשׁ	m. sg. abs. ptc. Paᶜᶜal (!) "being translated"

Exercise 11: Infinitive Forms in Various Conjugations

מִבְעֵא	pe. "to seek"	תַּקֻּפָה	pa. "to grow strong"
הִתְבְּהָלָה	hitpe. "to hasten"	הַשְׁכָּחָה	ha. "to find"
יַצָּבָא	"to make certain"	מֶעְבַּד	pe. "to do"

Exercise 12: Mixed Verb Forms (I)

שָׁמְעִין m. pl. abs. ptc. pe. of שׁמע "listening"	יִתְעֲבֵד 3 m. sg. impf. hitpe. of עבד "he will be made"
יִשְׁתַּמְּעוּן 3 m. pl. impf. hitpa. of שׁמע "they will obey"	מְכַפְּתִין m. pl. abs. ptc. pa. of כפת "bound"
הַרְגִּשׁוּ וְהַשְׁכַּחוּ 3 m. pl. pf. ha. of חשׁך/רגשׁ "they snuck up and found"	מִתְכַּנְּשִׁין m. pl. abs. ptc. hitpa. of כנשׁ "gathering together"
מַחְצְפָה f. sg. abs. ptc. ha. of חצף "being urgent"	מֵאמַר inf. pe. of אמר "to say"
יִשְׁפַּר 3 m. sg. impf. or jussive pe. of שׁפר "it will please/may it please"	קָרֵא m. sg. abs. ptc. pe. of קרא "crying"
יְמַחֵא 3 m. sg. impf. pa. of מחא "he will hinder"	פְּתִיחָן f. pl. abs. ptc. pe. of פתח "being open"
יָכֵל לְשֵׁיזָבוּת m. sg. ptc. pe. of יכל + prep. ל + inf. const. shapᶜel of עזב "he is able to save"	הֶחֱסִנוּ 3 m. pl. pf. ha. of חסן "they took possession"
יַחְסְנוּן 3 m. pl. impf. ha. of חסן "they will take possession"	מְשֵׁיזִב m. sg. abs. ptc. shapᶜel of עזב "delivering"
חַבִּלוּ 3. pl .m. pf. pa. of חבל or imp. m. pl. "they destroyed"/"destroy!"	תְּקְפַת 3 f. sg. pf. pe. of תקף "it (the king's heart) grew strong"
הַשְׁפֵּלְתְּ 2 m. sg. pf. ha. of שׁפל "you made low"	לְהִתְקְטָלָה prep. ל + inf. hitpe. of קטל "to be slain"

Exercise 13: Verbs with Suffixes

לָא חַבְּלוּנִי neg. + 3 m. pl. pf. pa. of חבל + 1 c. sg. suf. "they did not hurt me"	הַשְׁלְמַהּ 3 m. sg. pf. ha. of שלם + 3 f. sg. suf. "he finished it"
חַתְמַהּ 3 m. sg. pf. pe. of חתם + 3 f. sg. suf. "he sealed it"	יִשְׁאֲלֶנְכוֹן 3 m. sg. impf. pe. of שאל + 2 m. pl. suf. "he will ask you"/"require of you"
יְטַעֲמוּנֵּהּ 3 m. pl. impf. pa. of טעם + n.e. + 3 m. sg. suf. "they will feed him"	יְבַהֲלֻנֵּהּ 3 m. pl. impf. pa. of בהל + n.e. + 3 m. sg. suf. "they will scare him"
הַשְׁלְטָךְ 2 m. sg. pf. ha. of שלט + 2 m. sg. suf. "he made you lord"	הוֹדַעְתֶּנָא 2 m. sg. pf. ha. of ידע + 1 c. pl. suf. "you informed us"

Exercise 14: Weak Verbs

הַנְפֵּק 3 m. sg. pf. ha. of נפק "he brought"	הֲקֵימֵת 1 c. sg. pf. ha. of קום "I raised"
שָׁרִיו 3 m. pl. pf. pa. of שרה "they began"	מַנִּיתָ 2 m. sg. pf. pa. of מנה "you appointed"
בְּעֵינָא 1 c. pl. pf. pe. of בעה "we sought"	אֶתְכְּרִיַּת 3 f. sg. pf. hitpe. of כרה "it [my spirit] was troubled"
נַדַּת 3 f. sg. pf. pe. of נדד "it [his sleep] fled"	הוֹדַע 3 m. sg. pf. ha. of ידע "he informed"
שָׁמֵת 1 c. sg. pf. pe. of שים "I set up"	יְדֻרוּן 3 m. pl. impf. pe. of דור "they will dwell"
מַלִּל 3 m. sg. pf. pa. of מלל "he spoke"	תִּפְּלוּן 2 m. pl. impf. pe. of נפל "you will fall down"

Exercise 15: Weak Verbs/Special Verbs with Suffixes

הֲתִיבוּנָא 3 m. pl. pf. ha. of תוב + 1 c. pl. suf. "they replied to us" (lit. "returned to us")	בְּנָהִי 3 m. sg. pf. pe. of בנה + 3 m. sg. suf. "he built it [the temple]"
יִתְּנִנַּה 3 m. sg. impf. pe. of נתן + 3 f. sg. suf. "he will give it [the kingship]"	שְׁנוֹהִי 3 m. pl. pf. pe. of שנה + 3 m. sg. suf. "they [facial expressions] changed him"
הַחֲוֹנִי m. pl. imp. of חוה + 1 c. sg. suf. "show me!"	הוֹדַעְתַּנִי 2 m. sg. pf. ha. of ידע + 1 c. sg. suf. "you let me know"
יְחַוִּנַּה 3 m. sg. impf. pa. of חוה + n.e. + 3 f. sg. suf. "he will show it"	הַעֲלְנִי m. sg. imp. ha. of עלל + 1 c. sg. suf. "bring me in!"

Exercise 16: Mixed Forms (II)

תִּנְדַּע 2 m. sg./3 f. sg. impf. pe. of ידע, "you will know"	יְהִיבַת 3 f. sg. pf. Peʿil of יהב, "she/it was given"
לְמֶהָךְ prep. ל + inf. pe. of הלך, "in order to go"	תְּדוּשִׁנַּה 2 m. sg. impf. pe. of דוש + n.e. + 3 f. sg. suf. "it [the beast] will trample it [the land] down"
סָלְקָן f. pl. ptc. pe. of סלק, "going up"	יְהַעְדּוֹן 3 m. pl. impf. ha. of עדה, "they will take away"
יְקוּמוּן 3 m. pl. impf. pe. of קום, "they will rise"	הֲקֵימֶת 1 c. sg. pf. ha. of קום, "I raised"
לְהוֹדָעָה prep. ל + inf. ha. of ידע, "in order to inform"	הֳקִימַת 3 f. sg. pf. ho. of קום, "it [the beast] was raised up"
הֲוֵית 1 c. sg. pf. pe. of הוה, "I was"	הֵיתָיוּ 3 m. pl. pf. ho.[113] of אתה, "they were brought"

---

113. The ha. (active) form would be הַיְתִיוּ.

הֲתִיבוּנָא 3 m. pl. pf. ha. of תוב + 1 c. pl. suf. "they will reply to us"	שַׁנִּיו 3 m. pl. pf. pa. of שנה, "they changed"
לְהַשְׁנָיָה prep. ל + inf. ha. of שנה, "to change"	שָׁתֵה sg. abs. ptc. pe. of שתה, "drinking"
יִשְׁתַּנּוֹן 3 m. sg. impf. hitpa. of שנא "they will be changed"	סַתְרֵהּ 3 m. sg. pf. pe.[114] of סתר + 3 m. sg. suf. "he destroyed it"
הַנְעֵל 3 m. sg. pf. ha. of עלל, "he brought in"	בֱּנַיְתַהּ 1 c. sg. pf. pe. of בנה + 3 f. sg. suf. "I built it"

Exercise 17: Genitive Chains

רוּחַ אֱלָהִין קַדִּישִׁין "a spirit of the holy gods"; I, undetermined const. chain	מַלְכָּא דִּי בָבֶל "the king of Babylon"; II
פְּשַׁר מִלְּתָא "the interpretation of the word"; I, det. const.	מָאנַיָּא דִּי בֵית אֱלָהָא "the vessels of the house of God"; II and I
חֶזְוֵי רֵאשִׁי "the visions of my head"; I, det. const. chain (det. through the 1 c. sg. suf.)	אֱלָהֲהוֹן דִּי־שַׁדְרַךְ מֵישַׁךְ וַעֲבֵד נְגוֹ "the God of Shadrach, Meshach, and Abednego"; III (lit. "their God, that of . . .")
פַּסָּא דִּי־יְדָא "the palm of the hand"; II	שָׁרְשׁוֹהִי דִּי אִילָנָא "the roots of the tree"; III (lit. "its roots, that of the tree")

---

114. Since the second radical does not have a *dagesh forte*, most dictionaries list the form as Peʿal. However, סתר in BH typically occurs in the Piʿʿel, which could suggest that סַתְרֵהּ is a Paʿʿel.

Exercise 18: Impersonal Speech

1. וִיקָרָה הֶעְדִּיו מִנֵּה

Lit. "And honor they took away from him" ("His honor was taken away"; Dan 5:20)

2. וְכָרוֹזָא קָרֵא בְחָיִל לְכוֹן אָמְרִין עַמְמַיָּא אֻמַּיָּא וְלִשָּׁנַיָּא

Lit. "And the messenger said with force: 'To you they are saying, O nations, peoples, and tongues . . .'" ("'. . . 'You are commanded, O nations, peoples, and languages . . .'"; Dan 3:4)

3. אָתַיָּא וְתִמְהַיָּא דִּי עֲבַד עִמִּי אֱלָהָא עִלָּיָא שְׁפַר קָדָמַי לְהַחֲוָיָה

Lit. "The signs and wonders that he made with me, the highest God, it is pleasant before me to reveal" ("The signs and wonders that the highest God has worked for me I am pleased to reveal"; Dan 3:32)

4. וַאֲרוּ עִם־עֲנָנֵי שְׁמַיָּא כְּבַר אֱנָשׁ אָתֵה הֲוָה

וְעַד־עַתִּיק יוֹמַיָּא מְטָה וּקְדָמוֹהִי הַקְרְבוּהִי

Lit. "And behold, with the clouds of heaven like a human being one was coming, and he approached the Ancient of Days, and they brought him before him" (". . . he approached him and was brought before him"; Dan 7:13)

Exercise 19: Word Order

1. מַלְכְּתָא לָקֳבֵל מִלֵּי מַלְכָּא וְרַבְרְבָנוֹהִי לְבֵית מִשְׁתְּיָא עַלַּלַת

Lit. "*The queen*, because of the words of the king and his lords, the banquet hall *she entered*" (Dan 5:10). Subject and verb bracket the sentence.

2. וּבַיְתָה דְנָה סַתְרֵהּ וְעַמָּה הַגְלִי לְבָבֶל

Lit. "And *this house* he destroyed it, and *the people* he deported to Babylon" (Ezra 5:12). "This house" and "the people" are direct objects, highlighted through first position.

3. גֻּבְרַיָּא אִלֵּךְ לָא־שָׂמוּ עֲלָיִךְ מַלְכָּא טְעֵם

לֵאלָהָיִךְ לָא פָלְחִין

וּלְצֶלֶם דַּהֲבָא דִּי הֲקֵימְתָּ לָא סָגְדִין

"*These men do* not *pay heed* to you, O king.

Your gods they do not honor,

the golden statue that you erected they do not worship." (Dan 3:12)

The first sentence has subject-verb structure; each of the following two sentences emphasizes the direct object by placing it first.

4. אַנְתְּה מַלְכָּא רַעְיוֹנָךְ עַל־מִשְׁכְּבָךְ

סְלִקוּ מָה דִּי לֶהֱוֵא אַחֲרֵי דְנָה וְגָלֵא רָזַיָּא הוֹדְעָךְ מָה־דִי לֶהֱוֵא

וַאֲנָה לָא בְחָכְמָה דִּי־אִיתַי בִּי מִן־כָּל־חַיַּיָּא רָזָא דְנָה גֱּלִי לִי

"*As for you*, O king, your thoughts on your bed came up (about) what would be after this; and the one who reveals mysteries let you know what is to be. *As for me*, not through wisdom that is in me more than in any living being was this mystery revealed to me" (Dan 2:29–30). The two words with particular emphasis are the personal pronouns "you" and "me" (lit. "I"), which, however, are not the grammatical subjects.

Exercise 20: The Use of דִּי

1. וְדָנִיֵּאל עַל וּבְעָה מִן־מַלְכָּא דִּי זְמָן יִנְתֶּן־לֵהּ וּפִשְׁרָא לְהַחֲוָיָה לְמַלְכָּא

"And Daniel went in and requested *that* the king give him time to tell the king the interpretation"[115] (Dan 2:16). דִּי introduces an object clause.

2. וּדְנָה כְּתָבָא דִּי רְשִׁים מְנֵא מְנֵא תְּקֵל וּפַרְסִין

"And this is the writing *that* was inscribed: 'Mene, Mene, Teqel, Uparsin'" (Dan 5:25). דִּי introduces a relative clause.

3. יְדִיעַ לֶהֱוֵא לְמַלְכָּא דִּי יְהוּדָיֵא דִּי סְלִקוּ מִן־לְוָתָךְ עֲלֶינָא אֲתוֹ לִירוּשְׁלֶם

"May it be known to the king *that* the Jews *who* came up from you to us have gone to Jerusalem" (Ezra 4:12). The first דִּי introduces an object clause; the second introduces a relative clause.

4. כְּעַן מַלְכָּא תְּקִים אֱסָרָא וְתִרְשֻׁם כְּתָבָא דִּי לָא לְהַשְׁנָיָה כְּדָת־מָדַי וּפָרַס דִּי־לָא תֶעְדֵּא

"Now, O king, establish the decree and sign the document *so that* it cannot be changed, according to the law of the Medes and the Persians, *which* cannot be revoked" (Dan 6:9). The first דִּי introduces a purpose clause; the second introduces a relative clause.

---

115. The infinitive introduces a final clause ("in order to").

5. וְאַף שְׁמָהָתְהֹם שְׁאֵלְנָא לְּהֹם לְהֹודָעוּתָךְ דִּי נִכְתֻּב שֻׁם־גֻּבְרַיָּא דִּי בְרָאשֵׁיהֹם

"Also, we asked them their names in order to inform you *so that* we could write down the names" (lit. "name") of the men *who* were their leaders (lit. "at their heads"; Ezra 5:10). The first דִּי introduces a purpose clause; the second introduces a relative clause.

Exercise 21: Conjunctions

1. וְדָנִיֵּאל כְּדִי יְדַע דִּי־רְשִׁים כְּתָבָא עַל לְבַיְתֵהּ

"And Daniel, *when* he knew that the decree had been written, went into his house." (Dan 6:10)

2. חָזֵה הֲוֵית עַד דִּי כָרְסָוָן רְמִיו וְעַתִּיק יֹומִין יְתִב

"And I watched *until* thrones were set up and the Ancient of Days sat." (Dan 7:9)

3. יָדַע אֲנָה דִּי עִדָּנָא אַנְתּוּן זָבְנִין כָּל־קֳבֵל דִּי חֲזֵיתֹון דִּי אַזְדָּא מִנִּי מִלְּתָא

"I know that you are buying yourselves time *because* you have seen that the decree from me is firm [is a fact]." (Dan 2:8)

4. לָהֵן מִן־דִּי הַרְגִּזוּ אֲבָהֳתַנָא לֶאֱלָהּ שְׁמַיָּא יְהַב הִמֹּו בְּיַד נְבוּכַדְנֶצַּר מֶלֶךְ־בָּבֶל

"Therefore, *when* our fathers had angered the God of heaven, he gave them into the hand of Nebuchadnezzar, the king of Babylon." (Ezra 5:12)

5. כְּעַן יְדִיעַ לֶהֱוֵא לְמַלְכָּא דִּי הֵן קִרְיְתָא דָךְ תִּתְבְּנֵא וְשׁוּרַיָּה יִשְׁתַּכְלְלוּן מִנְדָּה לָא יִנְתְּנוּן

"So let it be known to the king that, *if* this city is rebuilt and its walls are finished, they will not pay tribute." (Ezra 4:13)

6. כָּל־עַם אֻמָּה וְלִשָּׁן דִּי־יֵאמַר שָׁלוּ עַל אֱלָהֲהֹון

דִּי־שַׁדְרַךְ מֵישַׁךְ וַעֲבֵד נְגֹוא הַדָּמִין יִתְעֲבֵד וּבַיְתֵהּ נְוָלִי

יִשְׁתַּוֵּה כָּל־קֳבֵל דִּי לָא אִיתַי אֱלָהּ אָחֳרָן דִּי־יִכֻּל לְהַצָּלָה כִּדְנָה

"Any people, nation, and language that speaks anything against the God of Shadrach, Meshach, and Abednego shall be torn into pieces, and their houses shall be turned into a dunghill, *because* there is no other God who can save in this way." (Dan 3:29)

Paradigms

THE PERFECT

Peʿal

sg.	3 m.	reg.: רְשַׁם, שְׁפַר, תְּקֵף, שְׁלֵט, קְרֵב, תְּוַהּ, שְׁלַח, עֲבַד, סְגִד, קְצַף, בְּנַס, שְׁאֵל, (+ 3 m. sg. suf.), חַתְמַהּ (+ 3 f. sg. suf.), סַתְרֵהּ, כְּתַב, טְאֵב, סְגַר, זְעֵק, בְּאֵשׁ, שְׁמַע
		I ᵓ : אֲזַל, אֲמַר
		I *n*: נְפַל, נְשָׂא, נְפַק
		I *w*: יְתִב, יְדַע, יְהַב
		II *ī/ū*: קָם , רָם, בָּת, שָׂמֵהּ (+ 3 m. sg. suf.)
		II=III: עַל
		III *y*: בְּנָהִי, (אֲתָא) אֲתָה, מְנָה, הֲוָה, (מְטָה) מְטָא, חֲזָה, רְבָה, בְּעָה (+ 3 m. sg. suf.)

3 f.	reg.:	בְּטֵלַת, סְלִקַת, תְּקֵפַת[116]
	I ʾ :	אֲמֶרֶת
	I *n*:	נֶפְקַת
	II *ū*:	סָפַת
	II=III:	נַדַּת, עֲלֵלַת
	III *y*:	עֲנָת, מְטָת, רְבָת, עֲבַדַת, מְלָת, הֲוָת, מְחָת
2 m.	reg.:	רְשַׁמְתָּ, עֲבַדְתְּ, תְּקֵפְתְּ
	I *w*:	יְדַעְתָּ, יְכֵלְתָּ, יְהַבְתְּ
	II *ī*:	שָׂמְתָּ
	III *y*:	רְבַית, חֲזַיְתָה, הֲוַיְתָ
2 f.		
1 c.	reg.:	קִרְבֵת, עַבְדֵת, שִׁמְעֵת
	I ʾ:	אַמְרֵת
	I *n*:	נִטְרֵת, נִטְלֵת
	I *w*:	יִדְעֵת
	II *ī*:	שָׂמֵת
	III *y*:	בְּנַיְתַהּ, חֲזֵית, צְבִית, הֲוֵית, חֲזֵית (+ 3 f. sg. suf.)

116. Unusual vowel pattern of a 3 f. sg. (Ezra 4:24).

pl.	3 m.	reg.: סְלִקוּ ,עֲבַדוּ ,שְׁלַחוּ ,כְּתַבוּ ,שְׁלִטוּ ,(קְרִיבוּ) קְרִבוּ
		I ʾ: אֲזַלוּ ,אֲמַרוּ ,אֲכַלוּ
		I n: נְפַקוּ ,נְפַלוּ
		I w: יְהַבוּ
		II ī/ū: קָמוּ ,שָׂמוּ
		II=III: דָּקוּ
		III y: שְׁנוֹהִי (+ 3 m. sg. suf.) ,שְׁנוֹ ,בְּנוֹ ,אֲתוֹ ,מְטוֹ ,רְמוֹ[117] ,אֶשְׁתִּיו ,הֲווֹ ,בְּעוֹ ,עֲנוֹ
	3 f.	I n: נְפַקָו
	2 m.	reg.: שְׁלַחְתּוּן
		III y: חֲזֵיתוּן
	2 f.	
	1 c.	reg.: שְׁאֶלְנָא ,שְׁלַחֲנָא ,מְלַחֲנָא
		I ʾ: אֲזַלְנָא ,אֲמַרְנָא
		III y: רְמֵינָא ,בְּעֵינָא

Peʿil

sg.	3 m.	reg.: כְּתִיב ,קְטִיל ,רְשִׁים ,שְׁלִיחַ, טְרִיד
		I w: (יְהַב) יְהִיב ,יְדִיעַ
		II ī: שִׂים
		III y: שְׁוִי ,קְרִי ,גְּלִי

117. With prosthetic א to form a full opening syllable.

	3 f.	reg.: קְטִילַת, נְטִילַת, פְּרִיסַת
		I *w*: יְהִיבַת
		II *ī*: שֵׂמַת
	2 m.	reg.: תְּקִילְתָּה
	2 f.	
	1 c.	
pl.	3 m.	reg.: פְּתִיחוּ, מְרִיטוּ, כְּפַתוּ
		I *w*: יְהִיבוּ
		III *y*: רְמִיו
	3 f.	
	2 m.	
	2 f.	
	1 c.	

Hitpeᶜel/ ᵓItpeᶜel

sg.	3 m.	reg.: הִשְׁתְּכַח
		III *y*: הִתְמְלִי
	3 f.	reg.: הִשְׁתְּכַחַת (אִתְגְּזַרת), הִתְגְּזֶרֶת
		III *y*: אֶתְכְּרִיַת
	2 m.	reg.: הִשְׁתְּכַחַתְּ
	2 f.	
	1 c.	
pl.	3 m.	reg.: אֶתְעֲקַרוּ, הִתְרְחִצוּ
	3 f.	reg.: אֶתְעֲקַרוּ

	2 m.	reg.: הִזְדְּמִנְתּוּן
	2 f.	
	1 c.	

Pacᶜel

sg.	3 m.	reg.: בָּרֵךְ, קַטֵּל, קַבֵּל, שַׁכֵּן II=III: מַלֵּל III y: מַנִּי, רַבִּי
	3 f.	
	2 m.	reg.: שַׁבַּחְתָּ, הַדַּרְתָּ III y: מַנִּיתָ
	2 f.	
	1 c.	reg.: בָּרְכֵת, שַׁבְּחֵת, הַדְּרֵת
pl.	3 m.	reg.: שַׁבַּחוּ, בַּקַּרוּ, בַּטִּלוּ, חַבְּלוּנִי (+ 1 c. sg. suf.) III y: שַׁנִּיו, שָׁרִיו
	3 f.	
	2 m.	
	2 f.	
	1 c.	

Hitpacᶜal/ ʾItpacᶜal

sg.	3 m.	reg.: הִתְחָרַךְ III y: הִתְנַבִּי
	3 f.	
	2 m.	
	2 f.	

	1 c.	
pl.	3 m.	reg.: הִתְנַדַּבוּ
		I *w*: אִתְיָעַטוּ
	3 f.	
	2 m.	
	2 f.	
	1 c.	

Hitpolel

sg.	3 m.	
	3 f.	
	2 m.	II *ū*: הִתְרוֹמַמְתָּ
	2 f.	
	1 c.	

Hapᶜel/ᵓApᶜel

sg.	3 m.	reg.: הַצְלַח, הַשְׁלְטֵהּ (+ 3 m. sg. suf.), הַשְׁלְמַהּ (+ 3 f. sg. suf.)
		I ᵓ: הֵימֵן
		I *n*: הַנְפֵּק
		I *y/w*: הֵיבֵל, הוֹדַע, הוֹתֵב, הוֹדְעָךְ (+ 2 m. sg. suf.)
		II *ū*: הֲתִיב, הֲקֵים, הֲקִימֵהּ / אֲקִימֵהּ (+ 3 m. sg. suf.)
		II=III: הַנְעֵל
		III y: הַגְלִי
		doubly weak: הַיְתִי (אתה)

	3 f.	II=III: הַדֵּקֶת
	2 m.	reg.: הַשְׁפֵּלְתְּ
		I *w*: הוֹדַעְתַּנִי (+ 1 c. sg. suf.), הוֹדַעְתֶּנָא (+ 1 c. pl. suf.)
		II *ū*: הֲקֵימְתָּ
	2 f.	
	1 c.	reg.: הַשְׁכַּחַת
		II *ū*: הֲקֵימֶת
pl.	3 m.	reg.: הַקְרְבוּהִי, הַקְרִבוּ, הַרְגִּזוּ, הֶחֱסִנוּ, הַשְׁכַּחוּ, הַרְגִּשׁוּ, הַכְרִזוּ, הַלְבִּישׁוּ (+ 3 m. sg. suf.)
		I *n*: הַנְפִּקוּ
		II *ū*: הֵתִיבוּנָא (+ 1 c. sg. suf.), הֲקִימוּ
		II=III: הַדִּקוּ
		III *y*: הֶעְדִּיו
		doubly weak: הַיְתִיו (אתה)
		special: הַסִּקוּ (סלק)
	3 f.	
	2 m.	
	2 f.	
	1 c.	reg.: הַשְׁכַּחְנָה
		I *w*: הוֹדַעְנָא

Shapᶜel

sg.	3 m.	I laryngeal: שֵׁיזִיב (עזב) II=III: שַׁכְלְלֵהּ (+ 3 m. sg. suf.) III *y*: שֵׁיצִיא
	3 f.	
	2 m.	
	2 f.	
	1 c.	
pl.	3 m.	II=III: שַׁכְלִלוּ
	3 f.	
	2 m.	
	2 f.	
	1 c.	

Hopᶜal

sg.	3 m.	I ʾ: הוּבַד I *n*: הֻנְחַת II=III: הֻעַל special: הֻסַּק (סלק)
	3 f.	reg.: הָתְקְנַת ,הָחָרְבַת I *w*: הוּסְפַת II *ū*: הָקִימַת doubly weak: הֵיתָיְת (אתה)
	2 m.	
	2 f.	

	1 c.	
pl.	3 m.	II=III: הַעֲלוּ doubly weak: הֵיתָיוּ (אתה)
	3 f.	
	2 m.	
	2 f.	
	1 c.	

THE IMPERFECT

Peᶜal

sg.	3 m.	reg.: יִסְגֻּד, יִשְׁמַע, יִמְטֵא, יִלְבַּשׁ, יִשְׁלַט, יִסְכַּר, יִשְׁאֲלֶנְכוֹן (+ n.e. + 2 pl. suf.), וִידַחֲלַנִּי (+ *waw* + n.e. + 1 c. sg. suf.)
		I ᵓ: יֵאכֻל, יֵאמַר
		I *n*: יִתְּנַהּ, יִפֵּל, יִנְתֵּן (+ n.e.+ 3 f. sg. suf.)
		I *y/w*: יֵיטַב, יִתֵּב, יוּכַל[118] (and יִכֻל)
		II *ū*: יְקוּם, יְתוּב
		III *y*: יִשְׁנֵא, יֶעְדֵּה, יִבְעֵה, יִצְבֵּא, יִקְרֵה, לֶהֱוֵא
		special form: יְהָךְ (הלך)
	3 f.	reg.: תִּשְׁלַט
		I ᵓ: תֵּאכֻל
		II *ū*: תְּדוּשִׁנַּהּ, תְּדוּר, תְּקוּם (+ n.e. + 3 f. sg. suf.)
		II=III: תְּרַע
		III *y*: תִּשְׁנֵא, תֶּעְדֵּא, תֶּהֱוֵא
	2 m.	reg.: תִּרְשַׁם, תִּשְׁלַט, תִּלְבַּשׁ
		I *n*: תִּנְתֵּן
		I *w*: תּוּכַל, תִּנְדַּע[119]
		III *y*: תִּקְנֵא
	2 f.	

118. Dan 2:10; perhaps a "Hebraic" form in the Aramaic text.
119. Dan 5:16. The Ketib looks like a Hebrew form; the Qere, however, suggests the (Aramaic) form תִּכּוּל.

	1 c.	I *w*: אֶנְדַּע
		III *y*: אֶבְעֵא, אֶקְרֵא
pl.	3 m.	reg.: reg. יְחַלְּפוּן, יִפְלְחוּן, יִסְגְּדוּן, יְבַהֲלַנִּי (+ n.e. + 1 c. sg. suf.)
		I *n*: יִנְתְּנוּן
		I *w*: יִנְדְּעוּן
		II *ū*: יְדֻרוּן, יְקוּמוּן
		III *y*: לֶהֱוֹן, יִבְנוֹן, יִקְרוֹן, יִשְׁתּוֹן
	3 f.	reg.: יִשְׁכְּנָן
	2 m.	reg.: תַּעַבְדוּן, תִּסְגְּדוּן, תִּשְׁמְעוּן
		I *n*: תִּפְּלוּן
	2 f.	
	1 c.	reg.: נִכְתֻּב, נִסְגֻּד
		I ʾ: נֵאמַר

Hitpeʿel/ ʾItpeʿel

sg.	3 m.	reg.: יִתְעֲבֵד
		I *n*: יִתְנְסַח
		I *w*: יִתְיְהִב
		II *ī/ū*: יִתְּזִין, יִתְּשָׂם
		III *y*: יִתְקְרִי, יִתְבְּנֵא, יִתְרְמֵא, יִתְמְחֵא

	3 f.	reg.: תִּשְׁתְּבֵק I *w*: תִּתְיְהֵב III *y*: תִּתְבְּנֵא
	2 m.	
	2 f.	
	1 c.	
pl.	3 m.	I *y/w*: יִתְיַהֲבוּן II *ī*: יִתְּשָׂמוּן
	3 f.	
	2 m.	reg.: תִּתְעַבְדוּן III *y*: תִּתְרְמוֹן
	2 f.	
	1 c.	

Paᶜᶜel

sg.	3 m.	reg.: יְבַקַּר II=III: יְמַלֵּל III *y*: יְבַלֵּא, יְמַחֵא, יְחַוֵּנַּהּ (+ n.e. + 3 f. sg. suf.), יְחַוּנַּנִי (+ n.e. + 1 c. sg. suf.)
	3 f.	
	2 m.	reg.: תְּקָרֵב
	2 f.	
	1 c.	III *y*: אֲחַוֵּא

pl.	3 m.	reg.: יְבַהֲלֻנֵּהּ ,יְקַבְּלוּן, יְטַעֲמוּן ,יְטַעֲמוּנֵּהּ (+ n.e. + 3 m. sg. suf.), יְשַׁמְּשׁוּנֵּהּ (+ n.e. + 3 m. sg. suf.) , יְבַהֲלֻנַּנִי (+ n.e. + 1 c. sg. suf.) (+ n.e. + 3 m. sg. suf.) III *y*: יְבַעוֹן ,יִשְׁנוֹן
	3 f.	
	2 m.	reg.: תְּקַבְּלוּן
	2 f.	
	1 c.	III *y*: נִחֱוֵא

Hitpaᶜᶜal

sg.	3 m.	reg.: יִצְטַבַּע III *y*: יִשְׁתַּוֵּה ,יִשְׁתַּנֵּא
	3 f.	reg.: תִּתְחַבַּל
	2 m.	
	2 f.	
	1 c.	
pl.	3 m.	reg.: יִשְׁתַּמְּעוּן III *y*: יִשְׁתַּנּוֹן
	3 f.	
	2 m.	
	2 f.	
	1 c.	

Hapᶜel

sg.	3 m.	reg.: יְהַשְׁפֵּל I *w*: יְהוֹדַע II *ū*: יָקִים, יְהָקֵים [120] III *y*: יְהַחֲוֵה, יְהַשְׁנֵא
	3 f.	I *n*: תְּהַנְזֵק II *ū*: תָּסֵיף II=III: תַּדְקִנַּהּ, תַּדִּק, תַּטְלֵל (+ n.e. + 3 f. sg. suf.)
	2 m.	reg.: תְּהַשְׁכַּח II *ū*: תְּקִים [121]
	2 f.	
	1 c.	I *y/w*: אֲהוֹדְעִנַּהּ (+ n.e. + 3 m. sg. suf.)
pl.	3 m.	reg.: יַחְלְפוּן, יַחְסְנוּן I ᵓ: יְהוֹבְדוּן I *w*: יְהוֹדְעַנִּי, יְהוֹדְעוּן (+ n.e. + 1 c. sg. suf.) II *ī/ū*: יַחִיטוּ, יַהֲתִיבוּן [122] III *y*: יְהַעְדּוּן
	3 f.	

---

120. Dan 2:44; 4:14. There is no sign of the Hapᶜel infix -*ha*- in this form.
121. Dan 6:9.
122. Final ן is missing in this case (Ezra 4:12).

	2 m.	I *w*: תְּהוֹדְעוּן, תְּהוֹדְעוּנַּנִי (+ n.e. + 1 c. sg. suf.) III *y*: תְּהַחֲוֻן, תְּהַחֲוֻנַּנִי (+ n.e. + 1 c. sg. suf.)
	2 f.	
	1 c.	reg.: נְהַשְׁכַּח III *y*: נְהַחֲוֵה

ʾIshtapʿal

pl.	3 m.	II=III: יִשְׁתַּכְלְלוּן
	3 f.	
	2 m.	
	2 f.	
	1 c.	

THE IMPERATIVE

Peᶜal

sg.	m.	reg.: פְּרֻק
		I ʾ: אֱמַר, אֱזֵל
		I *n*: שֵׂא
		I *w*: הַב, דַּע
		III *y*: חֱיִי
	f.	I ʾ: אֲכֻלִי
		II *ū*: קוּמִי
pl.	m.	reg.: שְׁבֻקוּ
		I ʾ: אֱמַרוּ
		I *n*: פֻּקוּ
		II *ī*: שִׂימוּ
		II=III: גֹדוּ
		III *y*: אֱתוֹ
	f.	

Paᶜᶜel

sg.	m.	III *y*: מֵנִי
	f.	

pl.	m.	reg.: בַּדַּרוּ, חַבְּלוּהִי (+ 3 m. sg. suf.) II=III: קַצִּצוּ
	f.	

Hapʿel/ ʾApʿel

sg.	m.	reg.: הַשְׁלֵם I *n*: אֲחֵת II=III: הַעֲלְנִי (+ 1 c. sg. suf.)
	f.	
pl.	m.	I *n*: אַתַּרוּ III *y*: הַחֲוֻנִי (+ 1 c. sg. suf.)
	f.	

THE JUSSIVE

Peˁal

sg.	m.	reg.: יִשְׁלַח, יִשְׁפַּר, יִשְׁגֵּא
		I ʾ: יֵאמַר
		III y: לֶהֱוֵא
		Special: יְהָךְ (הלך)
	f.	II=III: תְּנֻד
pl.	m.	
	f.	III y: לֶהֶוְיָן

Hitpeˁel

sg.	m.	reg.: יִתְעֲבֵד
		I w: יִתְיְהֵב
		III y: יִתְבְּנֵא, יִתְקְרֵי
	f.	
pl.	m.	
	f.	

Paˁˁel

sg.	m.	reg.: יְמַנַּ֫ר, אַל־יְבַהֲלָךְ (+ 2 m. sg. suf.), אַל־יְבַהֲלוּךְ (+ 2 m. sg. suf.)
	f.	
pl.	m.	
	f.	

Hitpaᶜᶜal

sg.	m.	reg.: יִתְבְּקַר
	f.	
pl.	m.	III *y*: אַל־יִשְׁתַּנּוֹ [123]
	f.	

Hapᶜel

sg.	m.	I ᵒ: אַל־תְּהוֹבֵד [124]
	f.	
pl.	m.	
	f.	

Shapᶜel

sg.	m.	יְשֵׁיזְבִנָּךְ (+ n.e. + 2 m. sg. suf.)
	f.	
pl.	m.	
	f.	

123. Dan 5:10, referring to זִיוָיִךְ "your splendor/complexion [pl. noun], let it not be changed."
124. Jussive form serves as negation of the imperative.

THE PARTICIPLE

Peʿal

sg.	m.	reg.: עֲבֵד ,חֲשֵׁל ,כָּהֵל ,שָׁאֵל ,נָגֵד ,נָפֵק ,דָּלִק ,פָּלַח ,בָּרֵךְ ,נְזִק ,קָטֵל ,צָבֵא
		I ʾ : אָנֵס ,אָמַר
		I *n*: נָחֵת
		I *w*: יָהֵב ,יָכִל ,יָדַע
		II *ū*: קָאֵם
		III *y*: קָרֵא ,דָּמֵה ,שָׁתֵה ,חָזֵה ,גָּלֵא ,בָּעֵא ,עָנֵה ,אָתֵה
	f.	reg.: בָּטְלָא ,עָבְדָה ,רָפְסָה ,כָּתְבָה
		I ʾ : אָכְלָה
		I *w*: יָכְלָה ,יָקְדָה
pl.	m.	reg.: פָּלְחִין ,סָגְדִין ,שָׁמְעִין ,דָּבְקָן ,זָבְנִין ,דָּבְחִין ,עָבְדִין ,דָּחֲלִין ,שָׁמְעִין ,כָּהֲלִין ,טָרְדִין ,חָשְׁחִין
		I ʾ : אָמְרִין
		I *n*: נָפְלִין נָפְקִין
		I *w*: יָתְבִין ,יָהֲבִין ,יָכְלִין ,יָדְעִין
		II *ī/ū*: דָּאֲרִין ,דָּאֲנִין ,קָאֲמִין ,זָאֲעִין
		II=III: עָלֲלִין
		III *y*: שָׂנְאָיךְ (+ 2 m. sg. suf.) שָׁנִין ,חָזַיִן ,עָנַיִן ,בָּנַיִן ,בָּעַיִן ,שָׁתַיִן
	f.	reg.: סָלְקָן ,נָקְשָׁן ,כָּתְבָן

Peʿil

sg.	m.	reg.: אֲזֵה, זְקִף, בְּרִיךְ, שְׁלֵם, גְּמִיר, שְׁלִיחַ, עֲשִׂית
		I w: יְדִיעַ
		III y: שְׁרָא, אֲזֵה, בְּנֵה, חֲזֵה
	f.	reg.: שְׁחִיתָה, דְּחִילָה, תְּבִירָה
pl.	m.	reg.: חֲשִׁיבִין, זְהִירִין
	f.	reg.: פְּתִיחָן

Hitpeʿel

sg.	m.	reg.: מִתְעֲבֵד
		I w: מִתְיְהֵב
		II ī: מִתְּשָׂם
		III y: מִתְבְּנֵא
	f.	reg.: מִתְעַבְדָא
		I w: מִתְיַהֲבָא
pl.	m.	I y/w: מִתְיַהֲבִין
	f.	

Pa^{cc}el

sg.	m.	reg.: מְפַשַּׁר, מְהַדַּר, מְהַלֵּךְ, מְשַׁבַּח
		II=III: מְמַלִּל, מְרָעַע, מְרוֹמֵם
		III *y*: מְצַלֵּא, מְשָׁרֵא
	f.	II=III: מְמַלְלָה
pl.	m.	reg.: מְסַעֲדִין, מְצַבְּעִין
		III *y*: מְצַלַּיִן
	f.	

Pa^{cc}al

sg.	m.	reg.: מְפָרַשׁ, מְעָרַב, מְבָרַךְ
	f.	III *y*: מְשַׁנְיָא
pl.	m.	reg.: מְכַפְּתִין
	f.	reg.: מְסַתְּרָתָא (det.)

Hitpa^{cc}al

sg.	m.	reg.: מִשְׂתַּכַּל, מִשְׁתַּדַּר, מִתְבְּהַל, מִתְעָרַב
		I *n*: מִתְנַדַּב, מִתְנַצַּח
		II=III: מִתְחַנַּן
	f.	I *n*: מִתְנַשְּׂאָה

pl.	m.	reg.: מִשְׁתַּבְּשִׁין, מִתְכַּנְּשִׁין, מִתְעָרְבִין, מִתְקַטְּלִין I *n*: מִתְנַדְּבִין III *y*: מִשְׁתָּרֵין
	f.	

Hapʿel

sg.	m.	reg.: מַצְלַח, מַשְׁפִּיל I ˀ : מְהֵימַן I *n*: מַצֵּל I *w*: מוֹדֵא, מְהוֹדֵא II *ū*: מָרִים, מְהָקֵים II=III: מְהַדֵּק III *y*: מַחָא, מְהַעְדֵּה, מְהַשְׁנֵא (root חיא)
	f.	reg.: מְהַחְצְפָה (מַחְצְפָה) I *n*: מְהַנְזְקָה II=III: מַדְּקָה (מַדֵּקָה)
pl.	m.	reg.: מַצְלְחִין, מְהַקְרְבִין, מְהַלְכִין I *w*: מְהוֹדְעִין
	f.	II *ū*: מְגִיחָן

Hapᶜal

sg.	m.	I ᶜ: מְהֵימַן	
	f.		
pl.	m.	I *n*: מְהַהֲתִין	
	f.		

Shapᶜel/Sapᶜel

sg.	m.	מְשֵׁיזֵב	
	f.		
pl.	m.	מְסוֹבְלִין	
	f.		

THE INFINITIVE

Infinitive forms are given here with their prepositions.

Peʿal

reg.	(+ 3 m. sg. suf.) כְּמִקְרְבֵהּ ,לְמֶעְבַּד ,לְמִשְׁרֵא ,לְמִפְשַׁר ,לְמִשְׁבַּק ,לְמִכְנַשׁ
I ʾ	לְמֵמַר
I n	לְמִנְתַּן
II=III	בְּמֵחַן
III y	כְּמִצְבְּיֵהּ [125], לְמִבְנֵא ,לְמֶחֱזֵא ,לְמִקְרֵא ,לְמִרְמֵא ,לְמִגְלָא ,לְמִבְעֵא (+ 3 m. sg. suf.)
doubly weak	(+ 3 m. sg. suf.) לְמֵזְיֵהּ ,(אזה) לְמֵזֵא ,(אתה) לְמֵתֵא
special form	לִמְהָךְ (from הלך)

Hitpeʿel

reg.	לְהִתְקְטָלָה ,בְּהִתְבְּהָלָה

Paʿʿel

reg.	לְחַבָּלָה ,לְבַקָּרָא ,לְבַטָּלָא ,לְתַקָּפָה ,לְכַפָּתָה ,לְקַטָּלָה
I n	לְנַסָּכָה
I w	לְיַצָּבָא
II ū	לְקַיָּמָה

125. Also attested as infinitive forms of בנה are לְמִבְנְיָה (Ezra 5:9) and לִבְּנֵא (5:3, 13).

Hitpa‘‘al

I *n*	הִתְנַדָּבוּת (const. form)

Hap‘el

reg.	לְהַשְׁמָדָה ,לְהַשְׁכָּחָה ,לְהַשְׁפָּלָה
I ᵓ	לְהוֹבָדָה
I *n*	לְהַצָּלוּתֵהּ ,לְהַנְזָקָה ,לְהַצָּלָה (+ 3 m. sg. suf.)
I *y/w*	לְהוֹדָעוּתָנִי ,לְהוֹדָעָה ,לְהֵיבָלָה (+ 1 c. sg. suf.), לְהוֹדְעוּתָךְ (+ 2 m. sg. suf.)
II *ū*	לַהֲתָבוּתָךְ ,לַהֲזָדָה (+ 2 m. sg. suf.), לַהֲקָמוּתֵהּ (+ 3 m. sg. suf.)
II=III	לְהֶעָלָה ,לְהַנְעָלָה (first form with, second form without, dissimilation)
III *y*	לְהַשְׁנָיָה ,לְהַחֲוָיָה
doubly weak	(אתה) לְהֵיתָיָה
special form	(סלק) לְהַנְסָקָה

Shap‘el

II=III	לְשַׁכְלָלָה
I laryngeal (עזב)	לְשֵׁיזָבוּתַנָא (+ 1 c. pl. suf.), לְשֵׁיזָבוּתֵהּ (+ 3 m. sg. suf.), לְשֵׁיזָבוּתָךְ (+ 2 m. sg. suf.)

9 780664 234249